Sales Success

Sales Success

Motivation From Today's Top Sales Coaches

Mark Bowser with
**Zig Ziglar • Tom Hopkins
Scott McKain**

Made for Success
PUBLISHING

Made For Success Publishing
P.O. Box 1775 Issaquah, WA 98027
www.MadeForSuccessPublishing.com

Distributed by Made For Success Publishing

Library of Congress Cataloging-in-Publication data
   Bowser, Mark
   Sales Success: Motivation from Today's Top Sales Coaches
   p. cm.

ISBN: 9781613397831

LCCN: 2015917093

Printed in the United States of America

For further information contact Made For Success Publishing
+14255266480 or email service@madeforsuccess.net

Table of Contents

Introduction

Welcome to *Sales Success*. You are about to embark on a journey that could change your selling life. How so? Only you will know for sure. But, you may double or triple your sales in the next twelve months based on what you are going to learn in this book.

Many times, it is the small changes that make all the difference in a selling career. It is knowing that last number of the combination lock that opens the vault leading to sales success.

This is no ordinary sales book. Many business books on the market today are written much like a text book…you know, like the ones we didn't want to read when we were in school. Well, *Sales Success* is different. Mark Bowser has written an inspiring story that weaves the selling lessons together into a complete selling system that will propel you to the top of your selling goals.

Mark has then assembled a team of the best sales trainers and authors in the world today. To be the best, you need to learn from the best. Through these top experts such as Scott McKain, Tom Hopkins, the late Zig Ziglar and many others, you will watch as our fictional mentor Digger Jones guides his young prodigy to the ultimate success in selling. Pretty soon, you realize that you are gaining as much as Digger's prodigy.

This is a great book. One that you are going to return to time and again in the years to come. Enjoy the journey…to your sales success!

Chris Widener

Preface

"How can you be so incompetent? One sale! One sale! How can you only make one sale in a month? That is ridiculous. It was a measly sale at that!" bellowed an extremely angry and frustrated sales manager. "Jack, if I don't see improvement soon, you are out of here."

"Not again," thought a very depressed, dejected Jack Blake. This was his third sales job in a year and he was failing again. "What is wrong with me?"

As Jack left his manager's office, he felt lost. He had no clue on how to improve. He had no clue on where to even start. "It wouldn't make any difference anyway," thought Jack.

Eleven months ago, Jack had entered the world of selling full of excitement. Now he just felt like giving up. He thought back to the previous eleven months, to that excitement he felt as he accepted that first job selling insurance.

When he graduated from college a year and a half ago, he had felt like the world was his. He thought he was ready. He graduated in the top ten percent of his class with a double BA in Marketing and Business Administration, so why wasn't he able to succeed at sales?

After taking a few weeks to travel and relax, Jack had taken a job as a sales representative for FSI Insurance Company. FSI is the third largest insurance company in the nation and very selective on whom they let represent them as a sales representative.

Jack has always been interested in sales and knew he was going to rip this industry up with success. Jack first became interested in sales when he sold grapefruits to earn money for a Florida baseball trip for his little league team. He had sold more grapefruits than anyone else and paid for his entire trip without having to get any money from his parents.

Jack's first month at FSI went extremely well. That month, he had the third most sales on the team, beating the numbers of many veterans. He sold his parents a policy, his uncle and aunt in Michigan, his cousin Susanne in Georgia, and a number of his friends.

However, from there it began to go downhill. His second month was mediocre. In fact, that is where he ended up in the team rankings. Smack dab in the middle. His third month was awful. He ended the month better than only one other sales person, and he knew that guy was going to be fired. Jack was only mildly surprised when he was fired too.

It didn't take Jack long to get another job though. He landed what appeared to be a lucrative position with the largest auto dealer in the area. He was now one of the select sales representatives for Frank's Auto World, which represented Toyota, Honda, Ford, and Volvo cars. Talk about variety. This should be easy. He is just glad they didn't ask about his previous job in the interview. Frank's Auto World was so impressed with his college career that they hired Jack on the spot.

Now, all Jack had to do was prove that he could sell....which he didn't. He sold only three cars in his first six weeks. In fact, that isn't quite true. He only sold two. The third sale came when a couple came in and bought a car in ten minutes. They were sold before they had walked on the lot. They knew the make, model, color, and features that they wanted. In fact, they knew more about that particular car than Jack did.

That was the highlight of Jack's life as a car sales professional. In his second six weeks with Frank's Auto World, Jack only sold one car. They let him go shortly after that. Now, it looked like the same thing was going to happen again.

Jack's current job was selling Professional Training DVD and Audio Programs for Success is Yours Incorporated to businesses and individuals. Jack loved the product. Every time he watched or listened to one of the programs, he got motivated and began to believe he could succeed too.

Jack's thoughts finally brought him back to the reality at hand. "It is just so hard," he thought. "Well, it is about 4:30 PM. I may as well go home, get a good night's sleep, and give it another try in the morning."

As Jack walked into the entry door of his dingy apartment building, he opened his mailbox. "Junk mail, junk mail, what is this?" It was a light green envelope that just had his name on it. Someone had obviously just dropped it into the mailbox.

As Jack opened the plain envelope, his stomach sank. It was from his landlady, Mrs. Norris. Mrs. Norris was a sweet lady around 65 years of age. She had lost her husband about three years ago and had been running the apartment building ever since. She had salt and pepper hair, a plump figure, and always wore a warm, caring demeanor on her face. More than once, Jack had enjoyed sitting with her on a warm, sunny afternoon on a bench under the old sweet gum tree adjacent to the apartment complex parking lot.

Mrs. Norris seemed to understand Jack's feelings about how hard of a struggle he was having with his job. She had always been so supportive. It was always comforting to talk with her.

As he opened the small envelope, he saw a short handwritten note inside it. Jack unfolded the note and began to read:

> *Dear Jack,*
>
> *I hate to write a note like this, but I really have no choice. I know how hard your job is for you right now and I understand you are under a lot of stress. However, I am trying to separate my personal feelings for you and run my apartment complex like a business.*
>
> *Please know that you are like a son to me and I love you very, very much. If you could at least show intent to pay your rent. You haven't paid anything for the last two months. Can you at least pay half of your rent this month? If not, I will have no choice but to ask you to move out.*
>
> *I am so sorry about this Jack.*
>
> *God bless,*
> *Mrs. Norris*

"Great." Jack said out loud in a muffled tone. He understood of course. He also was embarrassed. Where was he going to get $350 in the next two weeks? His entire rent was $700 a month, and he knew that would be almost impossible for him to get a hold of in just two weeks. If only he could make a couple of big sales in the next two weeks.

As Jack made his way upstairs to his one bedroom apartment, he felt as though he was totally alone. He felt no one completely understood...or at least cared. Jack knew these thoughts weren't true, but that is how he felt.

Sure, he could ask his parents to float him a little loan. But, he had done that before. He didn't want to do that again. He had to do this on his own. He had to figure out a way. For the first time in a long time, Jack began to feel the twinkle of a little determination.

He needed some air. Maybe a walk would clear his mind. As he thought about his parents, Jack knew where he needed to go to clear his mind. Jack's parents had given him a Christmas gift of a season pass to the Cincinnati Zoo. Jack loved the zoo. As a kid, they would go to the Cincinnati Zoo about once a week during the summer. It is a wonderful zoo and one with a good bit of history too. It is the second oldest zoo in the United States.

Jack only lived about two miles from the zoo. In fact, Jack has lived in the Cincy area all his life. He grew up in the beautiful Cincinnati suburb of Loveland, OH.

As Jack entered the zoo entrance gates, he could already feel a bit of the stress leave his body. He walked past the entrance and headed to his favorite spot, the gorilla exhibit. He loved the gorillas. They are so majestic with such strength but also such poise as they climb up the trees and other elements in their zoo home. Everything Jack wasn't and wanted to be.

Jack walked into the exhibit and his eyes immediately caught the big guy, one of the main attractions to the zoo itself. Sam, the large male gorilla, was huge. He was snorting and pacing for the crowd. As he did, his blackish, gray fur bristled. He was larger than most male silverbacks, and he ruled his kingdom without question. Such confidence. "Boy," thought Jack. "If I had just a tiny piece of Sam's confidence, I wouldn't be in this mess."

Jack moved to the series of benches directly in the middle of the exhibit and took a seat. It felt good to sit down. He hadn't realized how exhausted he was. For a moment, Jack closed his eyes and let the thoughts and stress ease from his weary presence.

Jack was knocked out of his inner reverie by a voice. The voice said, "Is this seat taken?" Jack looked up and said "What?" An older gentleman was looking down at Jack. The man must have been in his seventies, maybe even eighties. He had stark white hair with just a touch of black in the back. His skin was wrinkly with the miles of successful living behind him. He was wearing a pair of business casual style Khaki pants, a solid baby blue golf shirt with just a hint of a stripe, and stark white (looked like he just took them out of the box) tennis shoes. But his eyes, there was something about his blue eyes. They sparkled with an energy and aliveness that Jack had never seen before. The old man said again, "Is this seat taken?"

Jack shook off the cobwebs in his mind and remembered his manners. Jack gestured to the open seat next to him on the bench and said, "Ah, no. Please." Before Jack could get the words out, the old man sat down right next to him.

Now, Jack felt uncomfortable. He felt like this man could see through the façade he showed the world and peer directly to the depths of his starved, despaired soul. He felt as though the old man was staring at him. Jack just stared straight ahead and watched Sam down a banana in one big gulp. "Should I turn my head? Should I glance his way?" thought Jack. "I don't know. This is uncomfortable. What is with this guy?"

Finally, Jack took a slight glance toward the old man. The old man immediately said, "Powerful, isn't he? Such strength."

"What?" asked Jack.

"Sam, the gorilla. He has such powerful strength. If we all had such confidence, success would be inevitable."

Now, Jack was beginning to freak out. He had had those exact thoughts a few minutes ago. "Is this guy in my head? Who is this guy?" Jack's thoughts were going a mile a minute trying to connect this seemingly impossible puzzle of an old (or should he say odd?) man.

The old man held out his hand, "The names Digger; Digger Jones." Jack reached out in instinct and grabbed the old man's hand. He was shocked at the strength of the old man's handshake. It was firm, but not too firm. It was confident, but not arrogant. But those blue eyes were what really caught Jack's attention. He couldn't stop focusing on them. They were like a breath of sweet energy that burrowed their way into his soul. On arrival, a warm calm would envelope you down deep and soon encompass you with peace. Again, Jack thought, "Who is this guy?"

"So, what brings you to Sam's house today?" asked Digger.

"Oh, no reason."

"You don't seem like a man who came for no reason."

Jack sighed and reluctantly said, "Oh, I am having some trouble at work." Why was he opening up to this man? Who is this guy?

"Not enough sales, huh?"

"How did...how did you know? How did you even know that I am in sales?" stammered a now very freaked out Jack.

"That is why I am here."

"What do you mean that is why you are here?"

Digger looked at Jack with those piercing eyes and said in a calm, firm voice, "Jack, I have been sent to you. I can help you solve your challenge."

"Who sent him? My boss? Mrs. Norris?" Jack's inner thoughts were bombarding him with more questions…but no answers. "No, his boss didn't really care and Mrs. Norris didn't know he was at the zoo. And besides, how would she ever know a guy like this?"

"Who sent you?" Jack finally asked Digger.

A small smile formed on the corners of Digger's mouth. "Don't worry about that. Just know that I am here to help…and I can help you, Jack. Tell you what, meet me tomorrow morning at 7:45 AM at this address." Digger handed Jack a shredded, wrinkled up scrap of paper with an address scrolled on it. "The Cincinnati Chamber of Commerce is hosting an event. There is someone I want you to meet. Just be there at 7:45 and a ticket will be waiting for you. I will see you tomorrow." With that, the old man got up, smiled, and made his way out of the Gorilla exhibit.

As Jack bent down to tie his shoes the next morning, his thoughts continued to plague him. "What am I doing? Am I really going to this address? It is 6:30 AM. I could still be sleeping." Jack finished tying his black Dockers dress shoes and he stood up. Jack had put on his best suit. It was a charcoal gray suit with a red pinstripe. Jack didn't even know why he had put on his best suit. He just felt like…he was supposed to.

"Oh well," Jack said out loud to no one, "I am going. I have made my decision. This Digger guy might be nuts, but I am curious now."

Jack pulled into the parking lot at 7:32 AM. It was packed. "Man, a lot of people get up early around here," thought Jack. After driving around for a few minutes, Jack finally found a parking spot a mile away (or what seemed like a mile away).

Jack walked into the big front doors of the Blue Ash Convention Center. He had heard about this place, but had never stepped foot into it before. He had never had a need to…until now.

He walked up to a temporary table that had been set up in the middle of the entry area. The table had a sign hanging on the front that read "Pre-Purchased Tickets." Well, this must be the place. Jack gave them his name and no sooner, he had a ticket in his hand.

He looked down at the ticket and printed in big red letters were the words, "BREAKFAST WITH ZIG ZIGLAR."

14

Wow, Jack had heard of Zig. Zig was a master salesperson. He had an old cassette that his dad had given him. He hadn't listened to it for years. Zig is here? Maybe, this won't be a waste of time after all.

"Jack! Good morning, my friend." Digger came bounding up to Jack and grabbed his hand. "So glad you can make it. Do I have a *treat* for you. Follow me."

Digger looked awesome. He was wearing a perfectly tailored solid black suit. You could eat off his shoes they were so shiny. His tie was a bright red with a matching handkerchief that was just peeking out of his left breast jacket pocket. He was wearing beautifully hand-crafted cufflinks that had the initials "DJ" imprinted on them.

Digger led Jack past the crowd of people and through a set of double doors. They were headed back stage. "Are you sure it is okay for us to be back here?"

"Oh yea! Don't worry about it. I do this all the time." On that, Jack had no doubt.

They walked into a little room and there he was… Zig Ziglar. Digger bellowed, "Zig, you are looking *better than good* my friend."

"And, you clean up pretty well too. For the last few years, I have gotten so used to seeing you in a golf shirt and those ugly teal striped pants of yours. I was beginning to think that you didn't own a suit anymore," laughed Zig.

"Ha. Ha. Just because I still don't travel all over the place doesn't mean I don't work…some of the time."

They know each other. Who is this Digger Jones?

"Zig, I want you to meet a friend of mine. This is Jack Blake. Jack, this is Zig Ziglar."

"Good morning, young man. Are you sure you want to hang around this guy?" laughed Zig. "He might hurt your reputation."

"Ahh. Don't listen to this old coot, Jack. I am like an old pair of shoes."

"Nice to meet you, sir," said Jack.

"Well," started Digger. "Let me answer the question that is on your mind, Jack. 'How do Zig and I know each other?' We go way back. Years ago, we both got our start in sales in the cookware business. We sold the best pots and pans this side of the Mississippi. In fact, the best pots and pans on either side of the Mississippi. Zig was always trying to keep up with me. He was always ranked number two to my number one."

"If I remember correctly," started Zig in that southern draw of his, "those numbers were the other way around. But of course, your memory was always a little suspect Digger," razzed Zig.

"Number one or number two, makes no difference," said Digger.

"Yea, that is what the number two placed individual always says."

"Well, anyway, we were both good."

"On that, I can agree," chuckled Zig.

"Jack, the reason you are here, is that I want to start your training by you hearing from the master. Zig is the best. So, you may as well start with the best."

"What did he mean, 'your training?'" thought a confused Jack.

"Well, Zig, just wanted you to meet Jack. We'll get out of your hair so that you can finish prepping for your presentation."

"You're never in my hair, Digger. Incidentally, I still have more hair than you do too," Zig said with a small smile forming on the corners of his mouth.

"Ah, you old coot," bellowed Digger with a similar smile forming on the corners of his mouth.

As Digger and Jack walked back through the double doors into the lobby area, Jack hesitated, but forced the question out of his lips, "Digger what did you mean when you told Mr. Ziglar that you wanted me to learn from him to start my training? What training?"

"You are having trouble with your sales, right? Like I said yesterday, I was sent to you."

Not much more was said about it. In a way, Jack was relieved that he now had guidance and help. He still didn't understand this Digger Jones, but he was beginning to trust him...and he liked him.

Digger and Jack walked into the auditorium. It was large. It could seat probably 2,000 people. It was packed. At the front of the auditorium was a large stage. It was brilliantly lit. They walked down and took their seats on the third row right smack dab in front of the middle of the stage. These were great seats. Jack would have expected no less from Digger.

As soon as they were seated, a sharp-dressed woman probably in her mid-forties walked onto the stage. She was beaming with enthusiasm. She walked up to the lectern, which was right in front of Digger and Jack's seats. She began to speak.

"Good morning. Welcome to the Cincinnati USA Regional Chamber's exciting event, *Breakfast with Zig Ziglar.* As you know, Zig doesn't accept many speaking engagements anymore. We are thrilled and honored to have him here with us today. Without further ado, please welcome the one, the only, Mr. Zig Ziglar."

The crowd erupted into a standing ovation that sounded more like a freight train had just entered the auditorium. Zig walked out onto the stage. What poise. What enthusiasm. It was hard to believe he was in his eighties. He and Digger are a lot alike.

Zig shook the hand of the woman who introduced him, and he looked over the excited crowd. Zig began to speak.

Chapter One

Selling – The Proud Profession

By Zig Ziglar

As Zig was about to start his presentation, Digger leaned over and nudged his young friend sitting beside him. "You are going to love this Jack. Zig is the best. The absolute best."

With that, Zig started to speak.

---•••---

I was going to start our time together with a little story I tell that will knock your hair out, but I notice several of you fellows have already heard it. So I certainly won't go into that at this particular moment. So, let me simply start by saying that years and years ago I was flying on a plane, which incidentally is the general way I fly, and I was seated next to an old boy who I couldn't help but notice had his wedding band on the index finger of his left hand. Well, I commented on it by saying, "Fellow, I can't help but notice you got your wedding band on the wrong finger." He looked over at me and said with a slight grin on his face, "Yeah, I married the wrong woman."

Well, I don't know if he married the wrong woman, but I do know that most people have a lot of wrong ideas about what professional salespeople are, what they represent, what they do, and the contributions they make. So, let's start with some questions for each of us to think about. Do you believe that you sell a really good product or service? Do you know that your product or service solves a problem? Do you believe that when you sell a product or service that solves a problem you deserve a profit? Do you believe that if you sell for example two products that solve two problems that you deserve two profits?

Let me ask you another question that may sound a bit odd to you. Have you been in the world of selling for as long as a year? Now, do you still have every dime that you've ever earned in the profession of selling? However, do you have customers that are still using and benefiting from what you sold them a year ago, two years ago, ten years ago, or even longer? So, here is the big question. Who's the big winner, you or the customer? It is the customer, isn't it? So, then is the profession of selling something you do to somebody or for somebody? So, why would you ever hesitate doing something nice to someone when you know he/she will benefit for a long, long time?

One of the things that happens to me periodically is that somebody will be thinking they are paying me a compliment by saying, "I imagine you can sell anything to anyone." When that happens, I always tell them that they have just described a con artist. A professional salesperson cannot and will not sell anything unless he or she knows without a shadow of a doubt that the customer is the big winner in the transaction. That's what the professional salesperson does. The message is very clear: make certain the customer is the big winner if you are going to build a career in the world of selling. And, to do that, you must sell products, goods, or services, where you are absolutely clear that when you leave that customer, he/she is the big winner.

Now, I want to tell you I'm very proud to be a salesperson, and a lot of people don't realize this, but America was literally discovered by a salesperson. Not by any stretch of the imagination could you excuse Christopher Columbus of being a navigator. He was looking for India; he missed it by twelve thousand miles. Now, let me tell you, that is not navigation.

Well, he was an Italian in Spain. Now, that is way out of his territory. He only had one prospect to call on, and if they said no, he would have had to swim back home. He really had to do some selling. On the trip, he literally had to keep selling in order to keep sailing. Not only that, but he had to make a sale before he even got aboard the ships because Isabelle and Ferdinand of Spain kept saying to him, "Chris, the price is too high. We can't afford it." Now, that is the same thing your prospects have been saying to you.

Since I was not there, I am sure this isn't verbatim, but I can imagine the conversation went something like this. Chris locked eyes with Isabelle and said, "Look, Izzy, you got a string of beads around your neck. Why don't we take them down to the pawn shop and hawk them so that we can finance the deal that way?" Historically speaking, they literally had to make special arrangements in order to get the deal done. So, America was discovered by a salesperson. We were also populated by a salesperson. Sir Walter Rally toured the coffee houses of London persuading those people to leave the security of their homeland to go into a foreign land where you had no guarantee on anything at all, and because of his successful selling, people came in droves to America.

America was freed by a sales professional. His name was George Washington. If you are a sales manager, I want you to consider this. Washington had to do a super sales job. He said to prospective recruits, "Look, we're going to go to war against the most powerful nation on earth. They have a big army and a big navy. We are planning a rebellion and we are going to fight those people, and I have got to tell you, to be completely honest, if we win this war, I'm not going to be able to pay you; sorry about that. And if we lose it, they are going to hang you from the highest tree." Now, if you think that you have trouble recruiting, just think about ole George. I mean he really had to do a sales job. We were freed by a salesperson.

We expanded our territory by salespeople, Louis and Clark. The first 175 years after the American Revolution, we were still just on the verge of the Appalachian Mountains. Louis and Clark studied what the British had done so they set up trading posts, manned by salespeople, so that when people went westward they could get the supplies that were necessary. So, we were not only discovered by a salesperson, freed by a salesperson, populated by a salesperson, and expanded by salespeople, but today you as salespeople are completely responsible for goods and services you sell. Our whole economy depends on it.

Let me ask you another question. Are you required to have a little piece of paper that you write the order on when you make a sale? Most salespeople at one point or another have to use paper, is that not true? Well, you see, that paper didn't start out as paper. It started out as a tree. Now what had to happen was we had to go out into the woods, cut the tree down, and then haul it to the paper mill. Now, had you not made the sale, there'd be no need for that in the paper mill, and there are hundreds of people involved in manufacturing that tree into paper.

What happens is that you take part of your profits you made on the sale and you go to the grocery store and you buy a can of beans and the grocer says if you are going to buy my beans then I got to get some more. So, he goes to the wholesaler and says, "Hey, need more beans." The wholesaler says, if you're going to buy my beans, then I got to get some more, so he goes to the canner and says, "Need more beans." The canner says if you are going to buy my beans, then I got to get some more. The canner goes to the farmer and says, "Need more beans." The farmer says if you are going to buy my beans, then I got to raise some more, and to do that, I got to get me a new tractor because the one I got is all worn out. So, he goes down to the dealer and says, "Got to have a new tractor," and the dealer says to himself, "Man, if you are going to buy my tractor, then I got to go to the factory and get another one because this is the last one I got." So, he goes to the factory and the factory says if you're going to do that, I have to bring in iron, plastic, steel, aluminum, lead, zinc, rubber, and all of the things to manufacture that tractor, and every bit of that happened because one day you got out there and made a sale. And, let me tell you, friend, that's what you ought to tell people.

Our economy is dependent on that. Since the economy is dependent on it, understand that your character is a critically important part of all of this. I'm not talking about making a sale. I'm talking about making a sale so that you can make the next one, and the next one, and the next one, and the next one. That's why character is so important.

Years ago, I spent fifteen years selling heavy-duty waterless cookware. I was the number one salesperson in America working for the Salad Master Corporation out of Dallas, Texas. I never will forget one occasion in Columbia, South Carolina. My friend Bill was struggling. Now, Bill and I sold the same product. We were in different organizations, but we were friends, so we would frequently get together just to chat.

I was over at his house. I was really excited and there was Bill singing the blues. We were in his kitchen having a little chat. I mean things were tough, and as I got talking to him, I said, "Well, Bill, I know what your problem is"

He said, "What's my problem, man; tell me quick."

I said, "You're trying to sell something you don't believe in."

Well, he about exploded. He said, "What do you mean I don't believe in it? We have the greatest set of cookware on the American market."

I said, "I know that, Bill, but it's obvious you don't know it."

In a testy voice, Bill said, "What do you mean I don't believe in it? I left the company I was with for four years. I was a manager there, and I came aboard here as a salesperson because I believe in this product."

I made a little eye contact with the set of pots he had hanging over his stove…and they weren't our company's pots.

"Oh, that," said Bill. "But Zig, you know what my situation is. Man, I wrecked my car, and for about a month there, I had to depend on the bus and cabs in order to go make calls. You can't operate like that. And, you know my wife has been in the hospital. She was in there for ten days, and we didn't have any insurance. The hospital bill was horrendous. Now, it looks like we're going to have to put the boys in the hospital to get their tonsils out. But Zig, I am going to get a set of the cookware."

I then asked him how long he had been with our company. He said it had been five years. I then asked him what his excuse was last year for not having a set of the cookware. And the year before that and the year before that. I then looked right into his eyes and said, "Bill, let me tell you the thought process that takes place when you're in the closing situation and the prospect says to you, *'Bill I'd love to buy this set of cookware. It is really neat, but you see, I can't. I wrecked my car a month ago and my wife's been in the hospital for ten days and I don't have any insurance, and man, that just stripped us bare. Now it looks like we're going to have to put the boys in the hospital and get their tonsils out.'* I said, "Now Bill, you and I both know nobody is going to come up with exactly the same excuses that you came up with, but when they give you any excuse at all, you're sitting there saying to yourself quietly, *'Now think positive, Bill. Think positive'*, but deep down, what you're thinking is *'Yeah, I know exactly what you mean. That's the reason I don't have a set of the stuff myself.'*"

I let that sink in for a moment and then I told Bill that he needed to buy a set of the cookware from himself that day before he went out to make his first sales call. He asked me if I really thought it was that important. I told him I didn't think it would make a difference. I knew it would make a difference. I told Bill that if he did this, he would sell enough extra cookware that week to pay for his own set of cookware. Well, I made a sale that day. I persuaded Bill to buy a set of cookware off himself.

Later, he told me he earned more than enough to pay for his own set of cookware and acknowledged as he went on in his career that the best investment that he ever made was the investment in his own product. Owners are closers. Owners sell; that is the point I'm trying to get across. Believe in what you're selling enough that you would sell it to your mother or your daughter or your son or your dad. Believe it enough that you're using it yourself. Now, don't misunderstand. I don't think if you sell 747 airplanes that you have to buy a 747. But, if you're selling Fords and you're driving a Chevrolet, then there's something that's a little inconsistent about what you're talking about. Selling is a transference of feeling. Well, what I'm really getting at is character is the base on which you are believing. You see, the heart of the sale really does start with the honest factor, and that is what character is all about. You see, values determine behavior. Behavior determines reputation. Reputation determines advantages. It is so important.

A lot of people think that their lives are completely out of focus. That their lives are all filled up but they are not all filled up. They are just a little bit out of focus. As salespeople, we first need to focus on getting prospects. Then, we need to focus on getting appointments. Then, we need to focus on making the presentation. Then, we need to focus on getting them to take a positive action.

I can't tell you the number of times I've been on a sales call with a new salesperson who will be talking and talking and talking, and you know what? They still never asks for the order. I have, on occasion, heard the prospect say, "Now, you're not trying to sell me something, are you? "And believe it or not, the salesperson will say, "Oh, no, no, no." Well, what are you, a professional listener? I mean, as I understand it, the purpose of the call is to make the sale. That's why honesty and integrity are so important. The belief you have in your product or service will come out, and the depth of your sincerity is infinitely more persuasive than the height of your knowledge and all of these other things.

We are in the people business. This is where honesty comes in. You see, when you talk about integrity, there are some people who will say that everything is relative. I have never met the owner of a business who said he or she would hire an accountant or a treasurer who was only relatively honest. It just doesn't happen. When I go out of town and come back, my wife has never yet asked me if I have been relatively faithful while I was gone. There are some things that are right and there are some things that are wrong. You see, with integrity, you do the right thing and since you do the right thing then there is no guilt involved. With integrity, you have nothing to fear because you have nothing to hide. You can talk to your customers who you sold to yesterday and you can talk to them tomorrow, next week, or next year, because you know that in your heart that they are the big winners and that's where the integrity comes in. With integrity, you have no fear because you have nothing to hide. And since you have nothing to hide, you have no guilt. Get those two burdens, fear and guilt, off your shoulders and you will sell far more and you will sell it more freely.

Let me also point out that this has been validated by the Forum Corporation out of Boston, Massachusetts. They did a study on 341 sales people. One hundred and seventy-three of them were really super successful, and the other one hundred and sixty-eight were also good. They analyzed what makes the difference between the super successful and those who are good, and what they discovered was two major factors. Number one: those who had absolute integrity and believed that their word was their bond were much more likely to get the sale. My mama used to say to me, "If your word is no good, eventually you're no good either." Our words do determine so many things.

The second thing these super successful salespeople had was an understanding that the sale was not complete until the order had been signed, the merchandise, goods, or services had been delivered, and the customer was happy with the transaction. Only then can you truly say you have made the sale.

These are the customers that will send you to their friends and relatives in order to buy. These are the ones that give you the recommendations. Otherwise, you'll always have to be prospecting. And that's okay, but it's so much easier if you don't have to do that all the time because your happy customers have filled your pipeline with referrals.

Let me put it this way. We need to be so excited and so enthusiastic and so motivated about what we sell and what it will do for the prospect that everything else is completely out of focus. Instead, our focus needs to be on satisfying and meeting the customer's needs so that they will benefit as a result of it.

Why am I so excited about the profession of selling? Not only do we have so much control over the economy, but let me tell you something. I've seen people experience such incredible growth as they became successful in the world of selling. You have what it takes. You were created by God to be a winner.

I'm not talking about building a super inflated ego. You know, conceit is a weird disease that makes everyone sick except the one who has it. That is not what I am talking about. I am talking about building a healthy self-image. It was Muhammad Ali who said, "Just remember, that if man can take moldy bread and can make penicillin out of it, just consider what a loving God can make out of you." My friend, you were designed for accomplishment. You were engineered for success. You are endowed with the seeds of greatness.

What God has put inside of you is waiting to come out. Many times, all you have to do is wake up your potential inside. What I am saying is that we have to keep on growing. I'm a huge advocate of Automobile University. I just believe that it's the most important university in America. Listening to audio programs in your car can do so very much for you. Now, when you think about it, we spend hundreds of dollars every year dressing the outside of our bodies, such as the clothes, the haircuts, the shaves, and the goop we put on our hair. We spend thousands of dollars on our cars in order to get to our sales calls. But, how much do you invest on what goes into your head?

The question we have to ask ourselves is this: if we are willing to spend all this money to dress up the outside of ourselves before we make a sales call, doesn't it make sense to also know what to say when we get there? You see, that's where Automobile University comes in. I can't tell you over the years how many thousands of salespeople have said to me, "Zig, between calls I listened to those audio programs. I either listened to a new closing technique or a new motivational technique because if I just missed a sale, I want to be certain that I'm up for the next one." Bury that missed sell and go to the next one. I really do believe that the motivational teaching you receive in Automobile University does make a huge difference.

Another thing to keep in mind is that you need to keep listening and listening and listening to the same programs over and over again. When you've listened to it enough times so that you can finish the sentence before it is said, then it becomes self-talk. The most important conversation that you'll ever have is the conversation that you have with yourself. The most important opinion you have is the opinion that you have of yourself. Salespeople must keep growing. I love what Jim Rohn said. He said, "Formal education will earn you a living. Self-education will earn you a fortune." You see, you determine how much of a fortune you will earn by how much self-education you decide to get.

Why do I talk about listening over and over again? Why is repetition so important? A Stanford University study said this; oh, and by the way, I learned this in Automobile University. Stanford said that 95 percent of the people who hear, understand, and agree with a principle do not have the ability to apply it to their lives because they do not have the necessary resources. We are talking about three kinds of resources. Number one is the seminars that you attend. And we are delighted to have you with us here today. Number two is what you learn in Automobile University. And, number three is what you learn by reading. The investment of time and money you make in yourself will pay more dividends into your life than you could ever imagine.

Another thing we have to be aware of is that we need lots of energy to compete in the world of selling. We need an energy reserve. We need a physical reserve so we must eat right and exercise to take care of our bodies. We need to build that mental reserve, and that's the reason I keep talking about Automobile University. And then, we need to look into building that spiritual reserve. Now, I know in some areas, people say, "Wait a minute, Ziglar. We don't talk about that spiritual stuff around here." Well, that's too bad. You see, you're going to be dead a lot longer then you're going to be alive. So, we need some long-range goals. Let me just say this. I happen to believe that there's a lot of scientific evidence that supports my position. For example, the Dallas Morning News published an article back on February 12, 1996. It was an article about a study that was done by the Heritage Foundation. They discovered that regular worship service by the family reduces suicide, drug and alcohol abuse, crime, out of wedlock births, and divorce. People who go to church are far happier and healthier, they have a lower rate of depression, a higher self-esteem, longer and happier marriages, and can you believe what they put in the Dallas Morning News? They also have better sex. All I'm telling you is that it ain't a bad deal. Not only that, but these families earn an average of $11,000 more than those who do not go to church.

Incidentally, you won't be by yourself when you go to church because on any given Sunday, more people attend worship services than go to all the major league games all year long, plus all the NFL football games all year long, plus all the NBA basketball games all year long. And on Easter, it is not even close.

The last thing we are going to talk about, which we especially need in the world of selling, is the love and care for our prospect. I've often said that our values as sales professionals should be higher than anybody because we are trying to persuade people. You see, the con artist can persuade people to take action that is not in their best interest. If you have the best interest of your prospect in mind and you know what you have to offer in the form of your products and services is for their betterment, then you can sell with honest enthusiasm, close with conviction, and ask for the order with confidence. When you want them to buy because of what they will gain more than you want them to buy because of what you will gain… that's pure love. That's what it's all about. People don't really care how much you know, until they know how much you care about them.

Let me say it again; the minute you start to pull for them to buy for their benefit, you become more professional, more effective, more loving, and you'll sell much more. And you'll be able to go back and sell them again and again and again, and they'll be more than happy to send you to their friends and relatives. And when you do these things, you not just have a job in sales; you have a career in the world of selling, which in my opinion is the greatest profession in the world.

———————•●●•———————

Jack had never felt so energetic in his life. As he and Digger walked out of the auditorium into the bright, sunny, Cincinnati morning, Jack felt as though he could take on the world. Digger knew what he was feeling. Digger said, "You must now capitalize on the motivation you feel and the knowledge you have just gained. Here is a list of action steps I want you to ponder as you go make your sales calls today. Digger handed Jack a sheet of paper that read:

Digger Jones' Recommended Action Steps & Thoughts on *Selling-The Proud Profession*, by Zig Ziglar

1. Be proud of your profession. Selling is the most honorable and needed profession in the world. Remember, you help shape the economy.
2. Your character is the most important tool in your tool chest. Guard it and your word with your life…because they are.
3. Be sold yourself on what you sell. If you aren't, they won't either. Remember what Zig said: "Selling is a transference of feeling." Believing in what you sell creates passion, belief, and conviction. The prospect picks up on these elements more than anything else.
4. Selling is a people business. Today, we are in what is called Relationship Selling. Your first goal in selling is to build a relationship with the prospect. It has been said that with all things being equal, people buy from their friends. All things not being equal, people still buy from their friends.
5. Always have motivational and sales-related audio programs in your car. Listen and learn as you drive to your sales calls.
   Now, go out and make some sales.
                                                                    Digger Jones

Chapter Two

Highlights of the Perfect Sales Process

By Tom Hopkins

J ack and Digger walked into the beautifully expansive lobby of the Hilton in downtown Cincinnati. Jack looked up at the historic paintings that covered the cathedral ceilings.

"Well, you are in for a treat today," said Digger. "Many people have heard of a Mastermind Group, but very few take the time to be a part of one. These nine individuals you are about to meet have become for me my success cabinet. Any time I am stumped on a project or considering a new entrepreneur enterprise, I toss the idea first by these nine wise professionals."

"You see Jack, my nine friends and I form ten brains. Ten brains are better than one. We put our brains together and help create success for each other."

"I have read about the Mastermind Group in Napoleon Hill's book, but I have never experienced it," said Jack.

"Well, my young friend, I think you will be sold on the concept after today. Our group meets for two hours every other week. The first hour and fifteen minutes is spent brainstorming on two of the members' projects or challenges. The last forty-five minutes is dedicated to a presentation given by one of our members so that we can all improve our skills and knowledge. You see, my group consists of professionals in multiple different expertise. We have three Corporate CEOs, three Sales Professionals who are at the top of the profession, the CFO of a Fortune 50 company, two retired professionals including me, and even a Grammy-winning musician. This eclectic group of professionals forms, in my opinion, the best of the best Mastermind Group."

After all the introductions were given, it was time to start the meeting. It was fantastic. The thought energy in that room was like nothing Jack had ever experienced. He felt as though these ten people could solve all the world's problems if given the chance...well, at least some of the world's challenges.

Digger, of course, served as the chairperson of the meeting. At promptly one hour and 15 minutes into the meeting, Digger stood up and introduced the presenter for the day. "Alright friends, we have the privilege of learning today from one of the top sales producers of all time. His background comes from the real estate world. He holds the record for more houses sold in history. For the last couple of decades, or is it three, Tom?" Digger said with a twinkle in his eye. "Tom Hopkins is the Sales Champions Champion. He is the master of fundamentals. And as we know, fundamentals win championships. I give you...Tom Hopkins."

———————— •••• ————————

Tom walked up to the lectern as his colleagues gave him a warm welcome of applause. Tom began to speak:

Welcome to the Highlights of the Perfect Sales Process. As you know, the profession of selling consists of two components – finding the people to sell to and then of course selling the people you find. Awhile back, I came home from a tour, and I walked in on my wife working on a jigsaw puzzle. This took me by surprise because I hadn't seen her do this before. Now, I eat, breathe, and sleep selling, so everywhere I can find an analogy, find something that I can teach to better impact the student with the message, then I am all for it. I began thinking about puzzles. Let me ask you a question. When you begin to put a jigsaw puzzle together, where do you start? That's right, on the outside on a flat line, and you begin from the outside and work towards the middle. Well, the selling process is the same way. There are eight pieces you put together, and the end result is the perfect sales process.

Keeping with our puzzle analogy, the first piece on the outside in a corner is called **prospecting**. Now, nothing will ever replace eyeball-to-eyeball or belly-to-belly contact, that will always be the best, but today I decided to talk about **Activity in Different Areas**. That is the **first key to success in selling.**

30

Govern your entire life, not by productivity, which are sales, but by activities on a daily basis. Every day the number of quality activities you do, which are the contacts you make, will determine at the end of the month your success in the profession of selling. And so, I would like to talk about some types of prospecting that we really haven't discussed before, and that is first of all what we call working the warm market. A warm market is your friends, relatives, associates, and people you have worked with on an existing job. For example, when you leave a job and go into selling, I recommend that you develop a letter that introduces your new career to them. It lets them know you have chosen selling as a profession and that you would like them to help you build your business.

Now, here is an excellent example of an introductory letter that you might try sending to all of the people you know in your warm market. You might start like this:

Good morning Bob,

It is with great excitement that I inform you about a career change that I have recently made. I have just joined ABC Company as a Sales Executive, and it is my pleasure to introduce our company and its products and services to people in the community. Because of our relationship, Bob, I look forward to serving you and anyone you know in the area with the benefits this outstanding company provides. I will be in touch in the next few weeks to set a time to drop by and visit to see how I may serve you in the future.

Sincerely,

Your Name

If you send that letter to everyone you know, they will be ready when you call and arrange time to come by and visit with them. This is a wonderful way to start the process of activity and talking to more people about your product or service.

Many of you also will be assigned a territory where you are to go out into the community, meet businesses, and meet people working in the area, and you may want to establish a game plan for handling or sending an introductory letter to them. In fact, you might say something like this:

Good Morning Mr. Smith,

My name is Tom Hopkins, a representative of ABC Company. Upper management of my firm has given me an assignment....

Now I want you to notice the words I chose closely. By saying the words, "upper management has given me an assignment," you are almost blaming the company for the fact that you have to make this contact, thus the person you are contacting will have empathy for you and be more open when you call to set the time to visit. Then, you continue with the letter:

They have asked that I contact companies in this area to conduct a quick, two-question survey to enhance our ability to give better service to the clients we intend to serve. Thank you in advance for your help. I will be calling you in the next few weeks to set a time when we can visit.

By sending that letter, you will be amazed at how much warmer they are when you call and introduce yourself and mention to them that you have to come by to ask those two quick survey questions.

Another challenge we have is getting past the receptionists and secretaries, or otherwise known as the gatekeepers. In to4day's economy, gatekeepers are told with no uncertain terms to keep sales professionals like you and me away from the decision maker. The next time you run across a gatekeeper, I would love you to try this phraseology when you are attempting to get in to meet the decision maker. "Hello, my name is Tom Hopkins. I am in business in the community." Now, do not give the name of your company when you are making this type of call. You would then say, "I am calling regarding your (and you would state what your product or service does for the company. I am calling regarding your business machines, your copiers, your insurance programs, your employee benefits, what ever). Who in your company is responsible for that?" But, and this is very important, do not wait for their answer. I would like you then to insert the words, "by the way, who am I speaking with please?" When the receptionist gives his or her name, use this name and say "thank you for your help." You might even, if they do a very nice job on the phone, tell them what a nice job they do. Many receptionists and secretaries do not get a lot of recognition. I always tried to make anyone in any company that I was working with an ally by giving them recognition.

The **second piece in the puzzle is called Original Contact**. This is a process of meeting a person in such a way that something happens. It is the foundation of great selling, and remember, when you meet a person, you must radiate the goal of helping him/her want to like you, trust you, and want to listen to you. If you make that happen, you are on your way to great selling. Now, when you meet a person, there is a process called establishing rapport, which is fundamentally a way to get him/her to feel that you have something in common. Now, there are ways to do this. There are fundamentals. First of all, always use their name the way that they give it to you. Don't change their name; that can offend some people. Work on good eye contact, look them in the eyes, and yes, when people first see you, they should see you as a happy person. Give them a nice smile. I have also found it successful if you can find a way to give a sincere compliment, such as complementing the loveliness of their home or their offices. You can also compliment the job they do with their services, which creates value for the community.

Some of you may have a challenge remembering names; I know I did, so I started a habit and I would like to share it with you. When people give you their name, make a conscious effort to repeat their name in your mind four times. If their name is Bob Brown, as soon as they give it to you, repeat, Bob Brown, Bob Brown, Bob Brown, Bob Brown.

Another element to remember is the handshake. If you meet someone for the first time, then in my opinion, reaching out to shake his/her hand is too aggressive. I have a rule of thumb on the handshake – don't reach out unless it is a pre-planned visit, meaning they know who you are and why you are there; then there is nothing wrong with reaching out. Please, the business handshake for both men and women today is a deep firm handshake. People judge you often times by the way you come across in the very beginning with the handshake.

Next, we move on to the **third piece in the puzzle, which is Qualification.** The term qualification means we qualify them before we start asking/telling them about a future decision. We have created an acronym that will help you learn this concept. It is using the word "needs" spelled "n.e.a.d.s," meaning we are not going to talk about a future buying decision until we find out what their n.e.a.d.s. are. Now, this will make you unique in the profession of selling. Most salespeople right from the beginning tell the prospect that they know what they need, why they should buy it, and so forth. The problem with that is it is too pushy today. So, we are going to use the acronym, and each letter triggers one of the concepts of questioning and qualifying. The 'N' stands for the word 'now', meaning, what do they have now? Here is a key point. Their past buying experience somewhat dictates their future buying decisions. If you show me your past, I can tell you a lot about your future.

Once I know what you have now, or what your past experience is, I then want to probe with questions about what you 'enjoy', and that is what the 'E' stands for. What do they enjoy about what they have now? Why are they enjoying it? The reason why this is important is that they will want that same feature or an improvement of that feature in a new product.

The 'A' in N.E.A.D. stands for what they would like to 'alter'. That means what would the prospect like to do different or what would they like to change in the product or service?

The 'D' stands for 'decision maker'. It is vitally important that we as sales professionals find out who the real decision maker is for our prospect. You can do that with one wonderful little sentence. You can smile at the decision maker and say, "If we are fortunate to satisfy your needs, who other than yourself will be involved in the final decision?" That is a wonderful sentence for you to write down and start using.

The 'S' stands for 'solution'. As sales professionals, we are the solution to their need. We find out what that need is, and then we become the solution for it.

The **fourth in the puzzle is called Presentation.** Presentation, or demonstration, is the way that you show the benefits of your product. Never forget this: people do not invest in your product. They primarily invest in what it will do for them after they own it. In other words, my product is not what it is; my product is what it does and that is how the entire presentation must be structured.

There are fundamentals of a good presentation. First of all, presenting is not a spectator sport; it must be an involvement process where you involve the prospect in the presentation. Remember, the more senses that you get involved, the better. To do this, you must master the art of questioning. When you ask the prospect questions, you not only are building rapport, but you are also learning what their needs and concerns are. You are involving them in the presentation.

The presentation covers three basic fundamentals:

1. Who we are
2. What we have done
3. What we will do for you.

Now, when you finish your presentation, the next process is you are going to see how they feel about going further. We call this developing a little test question, and these two are so wonderful; I hope you will develop them. Just smile and say, "Mr. Johnson, how are you feeling about all of this so far?" What a great little question. It lets you know if they are ready to go further or if they have more questions.

The second question I would like you to consider is this: "Mr. Johnson, do you see why we are so excited about this product?" You see, if he says to you, "Yes, I am excited too," then he wants to go further and you know you are on target emotionally to get ready for the final closing of the sale.

At this point in the presentation, I can almost guarantee something is going to happen. Never forget, in most cases, no one can say "yes" until they first give you some type of no. In other words, there is something that happens when you present a product or service they don't own. They hear a little voice in their ear that says, "I want it, I want it, I want it," but then comes the fear of ownership. The buying tension grows. A pro knows how to turn the no into a yes. In fact, I do not believe we are really doing our job, the art of selling, until they say no or hit us with an area of concern. So, let me now cover the six steps of handling the objection.

Step Number 1 is what we call "Hear Them Out." In a nutshell, this simply means don't interrupt them. Too many people in selling, especially after they have a few years under their belt, answer objections too soon. They hear a couple of words that smell like an objection, so they jump in and end up answering the wrong area of concern. So, as a cardinal rule, I suggest you never attempt to answer an objection until the end of your presentation.

Use the, hear it twice rule. Now, what does that mean? Well, the prospect needs to mention the objection twice or it is probably not a real area of concern. So, if we are going to not answer a concern, we need to develop a concept I call the bypass. A bypass is simply asking them if it is ok if you wait to answer their question till the end of your presentation.

When they interrupt you with an objection and you are in the middle of the presentation, just simply say, "Mr. Johnson, I can appreciate that and I would like to note that as an area of concern, and with your permission, can I handle that at the end of my presentation?" Do you see how nice that was? Very gentle. The reason you use a bypass is two-fold. One, during your presentation you can address and overwhelm the objection to where it has no more power. Two, he may forget about the objection all together.

Step Number 2 is called 'Feed it Back'. That means we ask him to elaborate. All right, so what has happened here is that you have finished your presentation and sure enough, the prospect hits you with the same objection he hit you with earlier. Now, you know you have to handle it. He might say, for example, "Tom, I just really believe that it costs too much." And so you will feed it back. Warmly say – using his name – "John, today most things do; can you tell me about how much too much you feel it is?"

Step Number 3 is called 'Question It'. In this section, you simply question how important it is. Say, "Mr. Johnson, is this area of concern critical at arriving at a final decision?" This one question often eliminates the entire area of concern.

Step Number 4 is called 'Answer It'. This means you are choosing the applicable closing technique. Let me give you an analogy. Most of us have visited a restaurant where we first walk in, sit down, and then they hand us a menu. We open the menu and choose the food we want for the meal. In most cases, we aren't going to look up at the server and say, "I will have one of everything." Closing is the same way. We choose the applicable closing technique for the situation. So, you must have many closing techniques on your menu.

Step Number 5 is called 'Confirm the Answer'. When we have given our answer to the objection, we must then *Confirm the Answer*. That means you must now warmly say, "Now that settles that, doesn't it?" Now, if you don't do that, they will hit you with the same objection later on because you didn't confirm the fact that you answered it.

Step Number 6 is called 'Change Gears'. Change gears means when you handle an objection, you can't stop or they will hit you with another one. So, we take them elsewhere with three words. The words are, "By … the … way." Those three little words allow you now to take them mentally to a new subject.

And now, we are moving into the **sixth piece of the puzzle,** which is the most important piece in my opinion, which is **Closing a Sale.** You could call it 'calling for the final agreement'. You could call it 'getting the final *Yes*'. You see, never forget, if you have done everything else correctly up to now, the presentation should proceed smoothly and naturally to the close.

So, we have presented our benefits, we have shown the product, and now we must make a decision that they will own. This is called being assumptive that they will take advantage of the product or service. Never forget as you close the sale, you must close it with casual confidence. That means you must act relaxed. I know how nervous some of you get at this part of the selling process. That is why it is so important that you practice, drill, and rehearse your presentation so that it is not something new to you. It is something natural.

Now, when you go into the closing of the sale, do not show any physical or emotional change. Why? Because if you suddenly get different or sound different, it will trigger fear in them and they will put up their defenses. Remember, at this point you must have thoroughly covered the financial aspects. Why? Because people must know all the money involved before they can give you the final yes.

Closing of the sale begins with what we have always called the Order Blank Close, which is simply you ask them a question, they answer it, and you write it on your paperwork. It could be as simple as smiling and saying, "Mr. Johnson, what is the complete name of the company so I get it down properly?" If it is a husband and wife, those of you in personal sales, you might smile at the person who is really most excited about owning the product and just say, "Mary, did you have a middle initial?" You see, that is a reflex; they will give it to you without thinking. When they give you that middle initial or the correct spelling of the last name, or where they want the statements mailed, just nicely move on to your paperwork.

One of the scariest steps in the selling process for both the prospect and the sales professional is moving to the paperwork. But, we must move to the paperwork as soon and as natural as possible.

Oh, they might stop you as you begin to fill out the paperwork. This is natural and to be expected. The prospect might say something like, "Hang on, Tom. We aren't sure about this."

Just gently say, "I can understand that, Jim. What I thought I might do is put everything down, see how it looks, and then you can arrive at the right decision." See how gentle that is?

In fact, how many times will you hear "no" before you believe it? The top producers I have trained often times have to make a minimum of five attempts at closing a transaction before they get the final agreement. And, your ability to help them say "yes" when they want to say "no" will determine your success in selling. But, it is not overbearing, it's not strong, and it's not aggressive. It's done with questioning and a lot of empathy for them.

One more thing about paperwork. Don't just put your head down and start filling out the form like a dog chasing a rabbit down a rabbit hole. You will scare them to death. You must chit-chat with them as you fill out the form. Keep it loose. Keep it relaxed.

So, now what do we do? **The seventh piece in the puzzle is getting referrals**. Many people ask for referrals and don't get very many because they simply don't ask properly. I would like you to consider using the term "quality introductions" instead of the word "referral." You see, some people have been turned off when you ask for a referral. Why? Because they have had a bad experience in the past. They gave a friend's name as a referral, and as a result, their friend was upset.

Instead of asking for a referral, say something like this, "John, I am trying to build my business on a word-of-mouth basis, and I would so appreciate it if you could think of a couple people I might serve by giving me a couple of quality introductions."

When you ask for quality introductions, it is imperative that you bring up small groups of people they can think of. You might start with their closest friends, their family, and then you might ask about the people they work with, and so on. This helps spur on their memory, and you will be more successful at getting those "quality introductions."

I believe you will enhance your ability to get quality introductions if you build "thank you" notes into your business. I built my entire business through a referral base because I kept in touch with people and sent a lot of thank you notes. In our world today, which is getting so impersonal, those little hand-written thank you notes are worth their weight in gold.

A couple of new things I am teaching in which I highly recommend to you is that you take a few client names and addresses with you when you go out of state on a vacation. And...send them a postcard. It is so impressive. Write on the post card, "Hi Bob, I am getting a little rest so I can come back and give you better service than ever before. Thank you for being a valued client." You will be amazed at how open and nice they are when you return.

Another concept we are teaching is not to send the normal holiday cards. Everybody sends the normal holiday cards. I would like to suggest that you consider sending a Thanksgiving card or a letter, and it should say something like this, "During this season of Thanksgiving, let me thank you for being a valued client. We have so appreciated serving you and look forward to doing so for many years. We wish you a happy Thanksgiving, a joyous holiday season, and a prosperous new year." Now, you stand out. You are ahead of the competition. Try it! It works!

The foundation of the Perfect Sales Process is *attitude*. It is important that you work on your attitude every day. You got to keep it up and positive. Too many people in selling wait for a good client, a motivational seminar, a good book, or something else to get them motivated. The day you turn pro is the day that you realize that attitude in selling is everything. Attitude is something you have built within yourself. The most important thing you have is your enthusiasm, your excitement for the job that you do. And that is...serving people. Prospects will say "yes" to you more through your conviction, your excitement, and your enthusiasm than in anything else. And, if you do not have it in "here" (inside yourself), then you can't transmit it out "there."

So how do you get this attitude? Well, first of all, you have to do what I call "Mental Psych Up." Do this every day before you hit the streets of selling. This is how it works. Everyday, we all must get rid of the past. It is done. It is over. Get rid of it. You see, the past is like a bucket of ashes. What do you do with a bucket of ashes? You throw it out; you don't try to re-burn them. You get rid of it... Period! That is what you must do with the past. Every morning, make yourself a commitment, "I will live in the present moment."

By dwelling on the past, you are bringing those negative emotions and thoughts into the present. That determines your feelings and attitudes of today...which in turn determines your productivity of tomorrow. So by the negativity of yesterday, you are ruining your future. Let it go. Live in the present moment.

Another element that can devastate your attitude is a disease of the mind that tends to be prevalent in our country today. What disease am I talking about? Procrastination. You see, procrastination can be defined as living yesterday, avoiding today, and thus ruining tomorrow.

So, how do we overcome this challenge? By living by three little words: "DO IT NOW!" The things you don't enjoy, the things you want to avoid, the aspects of your selling day in which you can stand: DO THEM NOW! That is the key. Those are the actions that the sales champions do on a daily basis. It is my belief that the successful sales champions are willing to do the things the average salesperson is afraid of or unwilling to do. The sales champions do what they fear most, eliminating that fear and conquering procrastination.

Another element to keep in mind is a little philosophy we call *GOYA*. Those four letters stand for *Get Off Your Anatomy*. GOYA is the way out of any slump in selling. If all of the sudden sales are down, it is probably because 60-90 days ago your activity levels were lower, or you stopped doing the basic fundamentals that made you a success in selling in the first place. So, Get Off Your Anatomy and go back to the basics. Fundamentals win championships.

And finally my friends, I want you to realize something extremely important. One of the keys to a good attitude is to really be proud of what you do. The world of selling is arguably the most important job in America.

Almost every third world country and almost every other country is trying to duplicate our free market system. They want what we have, which is the freedom to produce a product or service and bring it to the consumer to make a profit. In a nutshell, they want the art form called selling. Selling is the highest paid hard work and the lowest paid easy work in the world today. Selling is without a doubt the foundation of our free enterprise system. It is what makes capitalism work. So, be proud of what you do. Walk with your shoulders back and your head held high because you have chosen the profession called selling. You have what it takes. Master this message and watch your sales soar as you fly to new heights as a champion.

"That was incredible," said Jack as he and Digger walked out of the Hilton onto the sun-lit street in downtown Cincinnati.

"My friend," said Digger. "You have now entered a bigger world. A world of not only your creativity…but also the creativity of your mastermind group. And, another thing I want you to consider, Jack, is that your mastermind group doesn't have to be just people you know."

"What do you mean?" asked Jack.

"Well, your mastermind group can also include the greatest minds of all time. We live in an amazing time in history where information is plentiful. And…the sad thing is that most people don't ever tap into it. For example, how many of your sales associates at your company listen to the personal development products your company sells?"

"As far as I know, none of them. We just sell them," said Jack.

"I can imagine your company charges a pretty hefty fee even for employees to access their personal development products." Digger said with a wry smile forming on the corners of his mouth.

"No, they don't charge us anything. They told us we could listen to anything we wanted," said Jack with a puzzled expression on his face as he looked into the eyes of his smiling mentor.

"Exactly!" exclaimed Digger.

As they approached Jack's car parked on the street, Digger paused and grabbed Jack on the arm. "Listen to me carefully, Jack. Success takes work. Work that most people aren't willing to do. People want the results of success…but none of the effort. But, if we are willing to put forth the effort, then we can make it come true. Walt Disney said, 'All our dreams can come true if we have the courage to pursue them.' The first thing you must do in pursuing your dream is to prepare for it. That takes learning. Learning that much of your competition isn't willing to do. That, my friend, gives you a distinct advantage."

With that, Digger reached into his pocket, pulled out a card, and handed it to Jack. On the card, it read in Digger's handwriting,

Jack,

I took the liberty of browsing through the list of products your company sells. Your company sells some of the best. As my eyes scanned the list, one jumped out to me as a perfect fit for you. It is Scott McKain's Distinctive Selling. If you want to succeed in the world of selling—and I know you do—then go through Scott's program.

Make it a Great Day! You can do it!

Digger

Chapter Three

Distinctive Selling

By Scott McKain

When Jack got home, he went to his laptop and booted it up. He jumped onto his company's website, logged in, and began scanning their list of training products. He went to the M's and found McKain. It listed an audio program and a video program. Jack put the computer cursor over "video" and clicked it.

After a few seconds, the screen changed to a view of a large stage. The crowd was applauding. Out walked a man, probably in his fifties. He wore black rimmed glasses and had a neatly trimmed beard. Jack settled into his chair as Scott McKain began to address his audience.

————————•●●•————————

No customer or prospect is ever going to be thrilled because the sales techniques you use are exactly like your competition.

There was a time not too long ago when Chevy owners felt superior to those poor souls driving Fords and vice versa. People gained identification through the goods that they purchased, the stores where they shopped, the institutions where they invested -- no matter the level of price or sophistication of the product.

However, over the past several years, we have seen the homogenization of practically everything. The car that I drive probably looks a lot like yours, no matter the nameplate. The big store where I shop almost certainly appears and feels a lot like where you do business. Where I bank and where you invest are most likely remarkably similar, no matter the logo on the door, no matter the community where it's located.

I would go as far as to suggest that many challenges that sales professionals encounter with customers spring from that central point: customers cannot determine a meaningful difference between you and your competitor for their business.

Please remember – customers always have to find a point of differentiation in order to make a decision. If there's no discernable advantage one way or another, then customers apply the ultimate differentiator: price.

Let's examine how we got in the mess – and, then I'll prescribe four specific strategies you can execute in order to stand out and move up, and sell distinctively.

There are three primary destroyers of differentiation. They are:

1. *Copycat competition*
2. *Technology has changed the customer*
3. *Familiarity breeds complacency*

Let's briefly examine each of these:

Destroyer #1: Copycat Competition

When my competitor creates a point of differentiation and gains an advantage – whether through a product or service...or individual selling skills – my natural inclination is to either:

*   Merely *imitate* the competition's improvement
*   Or, to attempt to *incrementally improve* upon their advancement

If you get slightly ahead of me with a new advancement or strategy, my natural response is to *replicate* it. If I can discover a method to duplicate your effort, it then becomes easy for my customer base -- and the team inside our organization -- to believe you no longer have a competitive advantage.

If your new method has enabled you to gain significant traction in the marketplace, then my best move appears to be to attempt to imitate whatever created your advantage, and attempt to *marginally do you one better* in order to compete with you in sales.

Notice the problem: in both examples, all efforts are based upon what my *competitor* is doing, not necessarily what my *customers* desire. And in most cases, such advancements are evolutionary -- not revolutionary.

Unfortunately, in many industries and in many cases, I am probably thinking I don't want to stick my neck out too far -- because you may chop it off in front of our customers and prospects. (Since we are competitors, *my* customers are *your* prospects and vice versa.) You feel the same way. The result is incremental, uninspiring advancement that appears to be "safe."

In the long run, however, this approach is anything *but* safe! Instead, what we are doing is destroying any points of differentiation that can better serve our customers, and enhance our sales results.

Destroyer #2: Technology Has Changed the Customer

A study by Accenture, (Investopedia, 2010), the global consulting firm, found that "73% of shoppers with smartphones favor using their smartphone to handle simple tasks in stores compared with 15% who favor interaction with an employee."

Roll that one around in your head for a bit. Almost three out of every four shoppers would prefer to stand in a store, pull out their iPhone or Android, and search for information, rather than to ask one of the sales professionals working there.

Why should I deal with a potentially "pushy" salesperson when I can obtain the information I need online? And, what could he or she tell me that a Google search can't?

This could be why, according to Reservoir Digital, (Resevoir Digital, 2013) an article in the Times of London reported that we used to average five visits to the showrooms of car dealers to make a decision on the purchase of an automobile – and now, the average has declined to *1.3.*

Author Daniel Pink explained this phenomenon in greater detail during an interview with National Public Radio (NPR, 2012):

> "Twenty years ago…when you walked into a Chevy dealer, the Chevy dealer knew a heck of a lot more about cars than you ever could ... you didn't have the adequate information. And so this is why we have the principle of 'caveat emptor' -- buyer beware. You gotta beware when the other guy knows a lot more than you.
>
> "Well, something curious has happened in the last 10 years in that you can walk into a car dealership with the invoice price of the car, something that even the salesmen/women at car dealers didn't know too long ago. And so in a world of information parity, or at least something close to it, we've moved -- 'caveat emptor' is still good advice, but equally good advice for the sellers is 'caveat venditor' -- seller beware."

How do you change the sales environment when your prospective customers *don't even want to talk to you?*

In other words, technology – from mobile smartphones to Google searches – has dramatically changed how customers think…and what customers *really* want.

Here is your primary opportunity: *You have to move from thinking about providing "information" to delivering "wisdom."*

In other words, while I may not need you for evidence and product specifications, I very well may find value when you can provide me with assistance and help. And, all you have to do is look at the difficulties of a few major sales organizations to understand the significance of this point.

Destroyer #3: Familiarity Breeds Complacency

One adage I heard often from my mom was *"familiarity breeds contempt."*

As much as I hate to dispute my mother's advice, my experience has taught me this one isn't true. If you become more familiar with someone, it does *not* automatically guarantee that you will become contemptuous of him or her.

When something like a product or service – or *you*, as a sales professional – is present to the point that you become thoroughly familiar and are boundlessly available, customers do not then begin to scorn it, hate it, or express disdain toward it.

Instead, we begin to *take you for granted*. We become *complacent* and presume you will always be around and that nothing is going to change (or improve).

We see this all the time in our personal lives. We, unfortunately, take for granted the people who are closest to us. We don't intend disrespect toward our spouses, for example. However, a steady drift toward complacency just seems to be a part of the human makeup.

Perhaps we presuppose if something or someone is overwhelmingly familiar, it represents a garden we no longer need to tend as enthusiastically or systematically. We erroneously assume, for example, that the love of our spouse will always be there on the vine, and it doesn't require as much nurturing, intensity, or the commitment of time that is demanded by something that we have yet to acquire.

Yet, it's not just the fact that your best and longest-term customers may be taking you and your efforts for granted. The fact is that you may be a bit complacent about their business, as well.

Every sales professional who I've met on the planet has some kind of *acquisition* strategy -- in other words, a plan for attracting *new* customers. (Some are good – others not – but all sales professionals want to acquire more sales. Isn't that part of the reason you're attending *this program*?)

However, fewer sales professionals have a *retention* strategy planned with the same degree of passion and precision; a precise program that outlines specific steps to retain current customers, while growing and expanding the business we are obtaining from them.

When we take something for granted, we no longer play as active a part in its growth and cultivation. If that happens in regards to a professional selling relationship, it often means that the association dies for lack of attention. For a sales professional, multiply that impact across a wide range of customers, and the result can be fatal for your career.

Consider this amalgamation of challenges:

- You are being copied by the competition – and perhaps you're doing the same to them – meaning customers have a harder time determining a meaningful difference between you
- A volatile economy
- Customers with more information than ever before, including facts and figures that were previously proprietary and often secret
- Your best customers taking you for granted -- and, vice versa

How could you possibly consider doing business in today's economic and competitive climate *without* selling in a distinctive manner?

Creating distinction in your marketplace -- and starting *now* -- is vital in creating the future you want in today's hyper-competitive sales economy.

The great news is that you can employ strategies that will build sales distinction immediately.

The Four Cornerstones of Distinction

Through my research and experience, I've discovered there are Four Cornerstones of Distinction. Every salesperson must draw upon these qualities to develop differentiation and uniqueness in the marketplace. These cornerstones will, at first, appear to be elemental. However, the more you study them -- and what it requires to be successful at each of these points -- the more you will realize how spectacularly challenging it is to execute them.

When you think about it, though, this paradox may also answer an important question: Why is it so rare to see *true* distinction in sales? The answer is that we:

1. Do not recognize or understand these cornerstones
2. Fail to develop and implement the strategies necessary to execute the cornerstones
3. Or, *both*

The great news, however, is that you can change this situation *instantly*. As you discover the Cornerstones of Distinction, you can immediately begin to plan how you will harness their power to become a more distinctive sales professional.

The Four Cornerstones of Distinction are:

- Clarity
- Creativity
- Communication
- Customer Experience Focus

Cornerstone #1: Clarity

I'm constantly asking sales professionals these important questions: "Who are you? How would you specifically define yourself and your company? What makes you distinctive in the marketplace? What are the advantages you have, from the customer's perspective?"

And guess what? *Most cannot answer the questions.*

By asking, "Who are you?" I do not mean your title, the company's name, or the name of the product you sell. The answer I'm seeking goes much, much deeper. I want to know what is compelling about you, what will create points of distinction about you, and what will establish a connection between us?

Here is the reason many -- and I suggest *most* -- sales professionals cannot answer the question: *they do not have clarity about who they really are…and what advantages they bring to the customer.*

Not as Easy as You Might Imagine

It's just flat-out difficult to discipline our organizations and ourselves to first discover, and then be clear about who and what we are. My experience is that it is *incredibly* more challenging than most companies and professionals anticipate.

Bob Engel, CEO of CoBank, supports this point enthusiastically. CoBank, based in Denver, is one of the 25 largest banks in the nation, and also moved into the Top 10 banks in the United States in terms of commercial and industrial lending. He recently told me his surprise about how difficult it was to be absolutely precise about the clarity of the organization -- even though surveys were showing employees were scoring the company high on its corporate mission.

Part of why Engel mentioned Clarity as such a difficult Cornerstone is that being clear about "who you are" also commands that you possess clarity about "who you are *not!*"

Clarity means you are precise about who you *are*—and just as exact about who you are *not!*

It is *easy* to stand upon generalities and modify them so you don't lose the attention of prospective customers.

In my experience, for example, many financial advisors have stated their practice focuses on a precise target so they may understand the specific needs of that respective group. Naturally, this approach would enable the advisors to provide a special and distinct service.

Then, however, people who fail to fit the target profile come along and want to invest—and the advisors take their business *anyway*!

When I ask them why they moved away from the clarity that would provide distinction, these sophisticated professionals have said in all seriousness, "But what if they win the lottery and I had turned them away?" Good grief! If that is now the standard, these advisors should start prospecting at convenience stores, because that is where most winning tickets are sold.

People always respond to this by asking me if this "clarity stuff" means a sales professional should turn away customers.

The answer is *yes!*

As you discover the other Cornerstones of Distinction, you will come to understand that truly differentiated sales professionals *never* try to attract everyone. Through their clarity, they take themselves out of the running for the business of some potential customers...which puts them in exactly the right position for their target market.

Don't get me wrong – I'm not talking about running away from...or ignoring...sales opportunities. I'm suggesting that Clarity is the first step in a strategy where we will attract customers, as well as pursue them. And, customers aren't attracted to a generic they can already obtain somewhere else.

I was involved in a series of consulting assignments with multimillion-dollar producers who are affiliated with the largest financial service brokerage in the country. As a result of the research developed with my good friend Dr. Rick Jensen of the Performance Center, located at PGA National Resort in Parkland, Florida, we know the highest performing financial advisors have developed highly specialized practices and extraordinary clarity regarding their points of distinction in the marketplace.

In eight separate meetings in a single day, I asked leading professionals in the field, "What differentiates your practice from those of other financial advisors?" Six times I received the response, "We provide great client service." Twice, the answer was, "I don't know."

Consider that for a moment; these are *successful* financial sales professionals! Granted, they may not be the absolute best of the best, but they aren't failures, either. Yet somehow they have missed the point that if they want to achieve higher levels of success and profitability, the most important step they can take is to make their practice differentiated from the scores of others in the same business.

Do they really think "great client service" is a differentiator? Does that mean that others in their industry are indicating they provide "pretty awful client service" to their investors? I doubt it.

The top financial advisors I have worked with are highly specialized. For example, they work *exclusively* with surgeons. Rick Jensen knows one professional who works only with PGA golfers -- and another who works only with people involved in the sport of polo.

If you have a pool of cash to invest, but are not a part of the polo scene, this advisor will refer you to someone else. (And, according to Dr. Jensen, he *has!*) By the way, Rick Jensen also reports that by turning away the business that is not a good fit, they have become among the most profitable of all professionals in their industry.

If I focus on surgeons, for example, as my clearly defined client base, I can learn their schedules, participate in their charitable activities, understand their unique professional challenges, educate myself in some of their specialized terminology, host client events that appeal to their specific needs, plan my work hours to fit the times that are easiest to contact them -- and be contacted by them -- and much more.

However, this also answers the question of why so few in the sales profession are able to attain significant distinction.

Can you begin to imagine how difficult it is to learn all of this and more about a specific customer base? Therefore, most sales professionals end up knowing their products, but not their customers. We're often a mile wide and an inch deep when it comes to knowing what would really make a difference for the very people we seek to serve. Or we try to serve so many that we end up truly engaging very few.

The truth is you don't have enough time or energy to create highly distinctive customer experiences for a widely varied assembly of wildly diverse customers.

On the other hand, you might say that Wal-Mart sells "everything to everybody" -- but that would not be accurate.

What if you want a tuxedo? What about a designer gown? You cannot find them at Wal-Mart. Marketing low prices every day on mass-market consumer items is clearly what Wal-Mart is all about. There is a sizable amount of clarity regarding who the company is, even though it handles thousands of items.

Part of the reason Clarity is so vital is: You cannot differentiate a generic.

Therefore, your goal is to be as precise as possible about who you are and what your organization is and what it is not. Be ready to fire prospects and customers who fail to fit your format.

Clarity is essential because those same customers asking, "Who are you?" will not present you with multiple opportunities to define yourself. After dealing with so many non-distinct organizations and professionals, they are vowing that they "won't get fooled again."

However, you can be clear about who and what you are -- and clearly be *boring*! If you cannot engage your customers and prospects, how can you expect them to perceive you have created sales distinction?

That's why it is critical to move to the second Cornerstone of Distinction: Creativity!

Cornerstone #2: Creativity

If you are going to inspire productive creativity -- the kind that can stimulate strategies that will have immediate positive impact upon your sales success -- here are the three action steps you should take.

Step One: Drive It Down

Your first step is to rely upon your clarity to break down all customer interaction into the smallest units or steps possible. Ask yourself this question: What is every point of contact a customer has with me, or my organization? Make an extremely detailed list.

It's time to be very specific about the process. If you are like most sales professionals -- you aren't finding too much in the way of differentiation.

For example, when a customer rents a car, it seems these are the twelve basic points of contact:

1. Call the agency (or travel agent) and make a reservation or use the Web site of the agency or travel company to secure a reservation.
2. Travel to the agency location by its bus (at the airport) or by transportation I arrange (for local locations).
3. Enter the agency and proceed to the counter.
4. Process paperwork and provide payment for the reservation.
5. Obtain driving directions.
6. Proceed to the rental car.
7. Exit the lot through security.
8. Drive the rental car for the period of my contract with the agency.
9. Return the car to the agency location.
10. Determine the final cost of rental based upon contract agreement and fuel level.
11. Complete car check-in.
12. Depart agency.

Your next step

The next step you should take should be to develop a similar list of the points of contact for:

- Your industry in general
- Your organization in particular

It's important that you drive this down to the most precise aspects possible. Every point of contact with your customer provides an opportunity for distinction!

Step Two: Pick a Point

Now that you know that every one of these specific items is an opening for you to create space from your competition, the next step is to review each point of contact to ascertain where you can develop sales differentiation.

Enterprise Rent-A-Car has been clear about what it is -- a company that rents automobiles. Yet when the company broke down the specific points of contact with customers, sales managers realized that at some point the renter has to obtain possession of the car. At other companies, customers must transport themselves to the rental locations, either at the airport or at a local office.

Not only did Enterprise follow the first two steps of driving it down and picking a point, the company followed through with step three.

Step Three: Develop a Difference

In 1957, Jack Taylor launched Enterprise Rent-A-Car from the lower level of a St. Louis car dealership.

By driving it down, picking a specific point -- the manner in which the customer gets to the product -- and developing a difference, Taylor's Enterprise has grown into the largest rental car company in America.

Enterprise realized the creative opportunity for differentiation. If all the company did was to incrementally improve their airport locations against its competition at Hertz and Avis, Enterprise probably would have remained trapped by the Three Destroyers of Differentiation, and in all likelihood, the company would have collapsed.

As it is, you can almost visualize the creative moment in a brainstorming meeting when someone said, "Wait a minute! What if we go to our customers? What if we take the car to them?" What differentiates Enterprise? You already know the answer: "At Enterprise, We Pick You Up."

By being creative -- within the boundaries of their established Clarity -- Enterprise developed a creative point of distinction.

You can do the same as a sales professional, if you just follow those three steps: Make a list of every point of contact you have with customers and prospects; pick a single point; develop a difference at that point.

The main point I want you to consider is that imitation usually generates neither passion nor distinction. If you are copying from others -- even if you are imitating the best in your field -- you are propagating a "me too" approach that will continue to cast you adrift on the sea of sameness. Creativity is the second cornerstone on the path to sales distinction!

Cornerstone #3: Communication

You and your organization probably have access to reams of data about what your customers are purchasing and why.

The problem is only a fraction of these assessments will provide real insight into how you can take your clarity -- now combined with creativity toward building unique and highly specific points of differentiation between you and your competitors -- and turn your information into communication that truly *connects* with your customers and prospects.

Legendary computer scientist Alan Kay, formerly of Disney and now head of the Viewpoints Research Institute, has said: "Why was Solomon recognized as the wisest man in the world? Because he knew more stories -- proverbs -- than anyone else. Scratch the surface in a typical boardroom and we're all just cavemen with briefcases, hungry for a wise person to tell us stories."

Dr. Kay is exactly right – a *story* is the connecting point that takes our clarity and creativity, and communicates our distinction in a manner that compels our customers and prospects to purchase from us.

We are story junkies. We get hooked on good stories. They can be scripted, as soap operas have demonstrated for decades before millions of viewers (and listeners in the days of radio) on a daily basis. The stories can be reality-based, as *Survivor* -- and the glut of imitators that have followed in the many years since -- has clearly proved.

It is no coincidence that these organizations that we are tired of hearing about -- Southwest, Starbucks, Apple, and so forth -- are the ones most frequently telling their stories in a precise and compelling manner.

So, why is it so difficult to find other examples? I suggest the reason is that so few sales professionals in business today understand the basics of telling the compelling story.

In today's hyper-connected world, customers have the ability to Google search the information – what they're desiring from you (as mentioned earlier) is wisdom! It's not that customers don't want facts, figures, and insight – it is that they want them delivered inside a wise, compelling story from you.

There are many great texts on creating and delivering great sales stories. (If you'd like to read more on crafting compelling narratives, read anything by Joseph Campbell.) In fact, the information is so readily available, there's no excuse for any sales professional to have failed to create an engaging narrative.

The old adage "build a better mousetrap and the world will beat a path to your door" is horribly incorrect and totally out of date. If the planet is unaware of your advantages -- and cannot Google the path to your doorway -- no one will ever arrive to obtain your product.

(Besides that, what customer "beats a path" to anyone's doorway? Just ship it to me overnight...)

If, however, you have developed *clarity* about who and what you are... and *creativity* that generates space between you and your competitors...and, if you have *communicated* those results through a compelling story tailored for the precise audiences you desire to attract...you have made major strides in developing the kind of distinction all organizations and professionals covet.

Yet, there is one remaining cornerstone! And it is the one that can propel you to greater sales heights than perhaps you ever imagined.

Cornerstone #4: Customer Experience Focus

Many, many years ago when I first started doing sales training programs, there was a line I used – as directed by the training company I was working for at that time – "Service is the first step to the next sale."

Looking back, I realize that statements just like that are part of the reason many of us in sales have failed to understand the importance of service, and the customer experience.

Here's the most important aspect for you to remember: Service...and the customer experience...is not just the first step to the next sale. It's a determining factor for THIS sale!

If you walked into a place of business as a customer, how would you feel if the salesperson said, "Hey...buy something from me, and THEN I'll take really good care of you!" Chances are, you'd find someplace else to spend your money! Customer expectations have enhanced, and the pressure upon us to create a distinctive customer experience begins the moment a prospect comes into contact with us.

Over the years, we have all heard the standard definitions for the *purpose of business*:

- *The purpose of business is to make a profit.*
- *The purpose of business is to obtain and retain customers profitably.*
- *Legendary management guru Peter Drucker said, "There is only one valid definition of business purpose: to create a customer."*

My meager attempt from my first book was simply this:

- *The purpose of any business is to profitably create experiences so compelling to customers their loyalty to your organization becomes assured.*

When your sales efforts -- and all of your organization's actions -- are wrapped up in "profitably creating experiences so compelling loyalty is assured," you have reached the point that this cornerstone advocates. It is the echelon where the customer's experience is at the center of every decision the organization makes – and every action that you take in distinctively converting prospects into customers.

To attain this level of performance, you need to create what I have been (for more than two decades) calling the "Ultimate Customer Experience ®" (UCE).

Creating the Ultimate Customer Experience ®

Step One: Ask a Question

The first step to create the UCE is to take a legal pad and (individually or with your team) ask this question:

"What would happen if *everything* went exactly right in the sales process?"

Then, record all of the responses.

Doing this is more complex than it might first appear. The single most important factor here is to keep drilling down to the smallest aspects of your interactions with customers and prospects. Constantly push for what would have to happen for that contact to be *exactly right*.

You must examine your interaction with your customers and prospects with extraordinary precision in order to get it perfect. That's the standard of the Ultimate Customer Experience ®.

Step Two: Engage Your Customer in the Process

When there is enhanced interaction, what follows is enhanced connectivity. Therefore, it is imperative you involve your customers in the process of creating the UCE. (After all, how can it be "ultimate" if it fails to deliver what the customer *really* wants?)

The most basic -- and often most powerful -- approach to involving the customer is simply to ask, "If you could describe the ultimate experience of doing business with an organization like ours (or a sales professional such as myself), what would that be?"

(Then...you *listen!*)

The fundamental challenge so many sales professionals experience with this approach is that *just listening* to the customer at this point seems counter-intuitive.

When a customer presents you with an answer, it provides an opportunity to initiate a transaction. Therefore, you may find it hard to resist the chance to "close the sale." For example, as your client answers your UCE question, she may state that she seeks something you already provide. Your natural inclination may be to butt in and say, *"We do that!"*

At this juncture, from the customer's perspective, this entire process immediately appears to be nothing more than a sales technique -- not an attempt to improve their customer experience.

And, this situation might additionally mean you (unintentionally) inhibit the relationship. Just as in your personal situations with friends and family, we know that customers desire to be listened to and appreciated. When you attempt to push the customer and close a transaction at this particular juncture, you may miss out on hearing highly insightful and revealing information.

Step Three: Sync the Information

Next, match the steps you have internally developed to create the UCE with the hopes and dreams that have been expressed through this process by your customers.

In some areas, the two may fit together quite nicely -- in other words, what the customers told you *they* wanted in the UCE, and what *you* outlined through the process, turn out to be highly similar.

However, I have also found some outcomes to be highly conflicting. If this is the case, realize that you are creating the UCE to engage *customers*! You must give *them* the benefit of the doubt.

On the other hand, you've got to temper this aspect with a point we've previously discussed: sometimes your vision of the future is more enhanced and profound than that of your customers. *Your* insight is required to build the UCE, as well.

Step Four: Outline the Roadblocks

Another question is vital to the development of the UCE: "What roadblocks prevent us from executing the UCE for every customer or prospect at every point of sales process?"

- Make a list of as many barriers as you can.
- Next, investigate and analyze each of them.

Some will be outdated corporate policies, while others will be misguided strategies. All of these UCE obstructions should be intensely scrutinized and, hopefully, eliminated. Remember, when you deliver UCEs...*sales grow!*

Step Five: Execute!

If only it were that simple, right?

Look, I know that none of us -- no matter our product, service, or sales position -- can just snap our fingers and put a thorough strategy into action.

Almost always, the Ultimate Customer Experience ® boils down to your commitment to deliver it during the sales process – and, by employees throughout your organization to make it happen in every aspect of the customer relationship.

It's critical to note: the Ultimate Customer Experience is an integral component in how distinctive professionals sell their products and services...every customer, every prospect, every time.

I have a considerable disagreement with a sales executive (whom I tremendously respect on a personal level) at a company where I have done a significant amount of work. He states, "We are primarily a sales organization. Our 'value add' of the customer experience enhances our access to customers and prospects and elevates our visibility in the marketplace. However, if someone on our team is hitting his or her numbers without using our customer experience program, then it's an optional resource for that person."

Here's the reason for my resistance to this line of thinking: Do you think Nordstrom managers would ever -- *in a million years* -- say to the sales team, "Look, if you are hitting your numbers in women's shoe sales, you can sell them any way you want?"

There is *zero* chance they would ever take that approach! Nordstrom would teach that its way of creating the experience and dealing with customers is just "how it's done." It is certainly not optional in any manner whatsoever. It is how the distinctive organization stimulates a distinctive sales process – one that has created incredibly loyal customers!

Every customer...every prospect...every time!

It All Comes Together . . .

Notice how all of the Cornerstones of Distinction are coming together?

The sales professional who will not develop clarity will find it enormously difficult to execute a strategy of customer-experience focus. If you haven't defined who and what you really are, it becomes impossible to deliver experiences to customers that are congruent with any degree of focus. (Obviously, because you don't *have* a focus!)

If you failed to be creative, and are therefore unsuccessful at communicating any points of distinction you've created, then the expectations of the prospect or customer aren't in alignment with a customer-experience focus.

Center your efforts on strategic differentiation in sales through a customer experience focus.

However, let's reverse the outlook to one that is positive:

- If you are clear about what you stand for, you can develop the precision necessary to deliver to admiring customers the kind of compelling experiences that ensure loyalty.
- You can communicate your individual and organizational distinction, in part because you're focused on customers, and because your actions are aligned. You truly "practice what you preach."
- The customer-experience focus is the right place for you to concentrate your efforts.

It is the final piece in the puzzle to build distinction as you differentiate yourself from your sales competition.

You Can Do It

The easiest tactic for you is to merely continue what you are currently doing. You may perceive that to "not make waves" and to "keep on keeping on" are the safest things for you to do. Let me emphatically state my belief that in the vast majority of cases, this is the most *dangerous* approach, no matter what you are selling.

Because of the Three Destroyers of Differentiation, your job in sales -- from an organizational and an individual perspective -- is only going to continue to *increase* in difficulty.

However, if you start today to chart a fresh approach based on the Four Cornerstones of Distinction, you can begin to enhance your sales results while you nurture and grow yourself into someone known both by your customers and in your industry for "distinctive selling."

Create differentiation. Sell distinctively.

It will make all the difference.

———————————•••••———————————

The video presentation had just ended and the phone rang in Jack's apartment. He walked over and picked up the line. "Hello."

"Hi Jack," said Digger. "What did you think of Scott's video presentation?"

"What? How did you know I just watched it?" stammered a surprised Jack.

"Oh, my boy. I know quite a few things. Tell me, what did you think about selling in a more distinctive way?"

"Well," said Jack with a pause to reflect. "I thought it made a lot of sense. That it is important not only to create a distinction between our products and services from our competitors, but to also create distinction in the way we sell to our prospects."

"Well," said Digger. "You chew on that for tonight and I will see you tomorrow. Good night."

With that, Digger was gone. Jack hung up the phone and gently shook his head as a gentle smile formed on his lips. He was beginning to get used to this very unique individual named Digger Jones.

Chapter Four

Creating Value First

By Mark Bowser

T he next morning, Jack went to meet Digger at Panera Bread. What a wonderful morning. Jack was pumped at the sale he had made yesterday afternoon.

At 7:15 AM, Jack walked into Panera Bread. As soon as he opened the door, he could smell the wonderful aroma of freshly brewed coffee and warm pastries. Oh, it smelled good.

Digger was sitting at a booth, waving at Jack. Jack walked over and sat down across from Digger. Jack immediately started speaking, "This stuff works. It really works. I closed a sale yesterday afternoon."

"This stuff does work," beamed a proud Digger. "Tell me all about the sale you made."

Digger listened intently as Jack excitedly told him about his successful experience of the day before. When he was finished, Digger said, "Great job. That is only the beginning. And, only the beginning of your education. I am going to go get us some breakfast. As I do, I want you to read this article by Mark Bowser." Digger handed Jack a newspaper and stood up to get in line.

Jack looked at the newspaper and began to read:

----------•●●●•----------

How are sales going? Do you have more prospects than you have time to call on today? Is your sales pipeline full, or are you hoping to bump into someone today who might possibly, just maybe, want to buy what you sell? Well, wherever you are on the spectrum, this column will share with you some simple ideas of expanding your list of prospects and customers.

Here is the key: Create value first! Simple, right? You don't think so? Well, here is why it is so important. Creating value first lessens the resistance from the prospective customer. Ponder this. It is a way that you can prove to them how well you can serve them…before they buy. So, how do you do this? Quite simply. Give something of value away. Really! It is that simple. Give value to a lot of people, and a lot of people will be knocking on your door.

What do you have that you can give away? Maybe you can give away a free sample, a free newsletter, a free consultation, etc… Here is an example. My chiropractor sells very effectively by giving away a coupon for a free body scan. Do you know where he prints this coupon? On the back of his business card. Every time he gives out one of his business cards, he is also giving away a free body scan. What does the body scan do? It creates value. Why? Because the only people who will use the coupon are ones who are having some sort of physical challenge or pain, such as in their back. This makes them a prospect for my doctor instead of just a suspect. Then, he gives them value with the body scan, which helps him diagnose the issue that is causing them pain and gives him insight on how to solve their pain. Value first…leads to sales.

Let me give you another example. Let's suppose you sell audio and DVD training programs. What if you gave away a free MP3 training program? How much would that cost you? Virtually nothing because you can create an MP3 from an existing product. Do you see where I am going with this? It costs you virtually nothing but…creates tremendous value for the prospective customer.

Maybe you run a local printing company. What if you offered 250 free business cards just to try out your business? That little investment may come back to you in droves.

Here is a way you could supercharge those ideas. What if you gave the coupon for a discount or a free MP3 training program to the Sales Manager at ABC Company and encouraged him/her to pass it out to all of his/her sales representatives? What if the chiropractor gave the coupon for a free body scan to the Human Resources Manager and encouraged him/her to give it to all the employees at ABC Company? The potential is endless.

As a Sales Trainer and Professional Speaker, I sometimes will give out free 45-minute preview seminars. It lets prospects test drive a seminar before they invest in a full seminar. I give them value by giving them ideas that they can use to be more prosperous. Does it work? Oh yea! For example, I booked multiple days of seminars with one client using this technique.

As an author, I give away free books. It is an important part of our selling strategy. The free books let the reader test drive my writing. If they enjoy it and benefit from it, guess what? They buy one of the other books. And the cycle goes on and on and on!

So, what are you waiting for? Put down that newspaper and go out and create some value today.

———————•●●●•———————

As Jack put down the article, Digger was arriving with their breakfast. "It looks like you are deep in thought," said Digger.

"I am just thinking about that article. On how... I can create value first."

"That is the key," smiled Digger. "Create a lot of value first...and you will never need to worry about keeping your sales pipeline full."

Chapter Five

Becoming More Persuasive

By Dr. Tony Alessandra

J ack pulled back into his apartment complex around 5:45 PM. He felt good about his day. He made one sale of about 150 sets of Zig Ziglar's *Strategies For Success* DVD/CD package. "That will be a nice commission," he thought to himself. He also felt good because he knew this product was really going to help his client. He also had planted some very promising seeds, and he knew some sales were going to grow from them. Life was beginning to turn around…and it felt good.

Jack decided to pop into the stereo DVD player one of his many samples of training resources that he sold. He decided on Dr. Tony Alessandra's program, *Becoming More Persuasive.* As Dr. Alessandra began to speak, Jack went into his tiny kitchen to prepare himself some dinner. Dr. Tony began:

———————•●●●•———————

Suppose you take your boss aside to tell him about your great idea for a new software product. It's an offshoot of your firm's present line, and one you're sure could be easily produced, thus nailing down a profitable niche. You expect him to be as jazzed about it as you are. Instead, he raises reservations about staff and funding. He voices doubts about timing and market. He questions whether the needed equipment and raw materials are available and, even if they are, whether foreign competitors wouldn't soon catch on and make the same product more cheaply. All in all, his response sounds suspiciously like a brush-off.

Why? Why are so many new ideas a tough sell? Isn't it true, as the old saying goes, that if you invent a better mousetrap, the world will beat a path to your door? No, that's baloney! In fact, it's never been less true – for a variety of reasons. For starters, people everywhere have become more savvy, skeptical, and even cynical. We've all become more jaded about advertising, more suspicious of political claims, and less trusting of those who bring us a message, any message – even one that may be in our best interest.

Second, organizations build barriers to change. Change entails risks, and risk conflicts with the desire for control and predictability. Change also requires approval by a lot of people, people with differing needs and interests. Third, and most important for our talk today, many people just aren't skilled at the art of persuading. No matter how brilliant your idea, no matter how technically advanced or economically sound it may be, it'll go nowhere unless you get others to go along with it. And the only way you do that is by persuading them, by communicating clearly why they really should want to do what you really need done.

The Art of Persuading

John Naisbitt, the futurist author of Megatrends 2000, said our high-tech capabilities have outpaced our "high-touch needs." In other words, we spend more and more time learning new technology and less and less time developing the interpersonal skills needed to explain an idea's worth. As a result, learning to improve our persuasiveness is both easier and harder than it used to be. Easier because we've now got email and voice mail, CD-ROMs and cellular phones, satellites and skywriting, and a vast array of other tools for communicating. But it's also more difficult, because the deluge of messages and ill-equipped messengers through all these forms cheapens them all. So nowadays, it's more crucial than ever to hone the skills that heighten our power of persuasion and, in turn, our charisma.

We're All Persuaders

The truth is, we're all involved in persuasion of some sort every day. If you're in sales, the use of persuasion is pretty obvious: you try to convince others to buy your product or service. But in our social and personal lives, too, there's a more subtle but almost constant use of persuasion as you seek a date, debate politics, try to talk your way out of a parking ticket, decide which video you and a friend will rent, or just make the case that yams, not mashed potatoes, will go better with that Thanksgiving turkey.

But sometimes the process of persuasion is more long term and less obvious than that. Take recycling. Twenty years ago, most people would have thought it was too much of a hassle to keep piles of empty bottles, aluminum cans, or old newspapers in some corner of their home. Today, a great many people recycle, or at least agree that it's a good idea to recycle.

What made us change? A couple decades of persistent persuasion from people in the ecology movement, from companies who care about the environment, and from our friends and neighbors who demonstrate how easy and worthwhile recycling can be. What's in it for us, they said in effect, is that the benefit greatly outweighs the cost, we can help save the earth's precious resources by just tossing bottles and cans in a couple bins in our garage.

The Four-Step Process

How can you improve your persuasiveness – and thus increase your personal connections? Well, a starting point is to make sure you and others understand the "need gap." The need gap is the difference between the current situation and the desired situation. Whatever the specifics of a situation, when other people perceive a gap you've cited – a "because" – there's a natural desire to want to fill it.

Here are four steps for determining, and then closing, the need gap and using it as a tool for persuasion. By the way, this tool is universal. It can be applied to large social issues, say, birth control or economic justice, or to more day-to-day challenges such as influencing your customers.

Here's the process:

1. Explore needs and goals
2. Create and select a solution
3. Commit to an action plan
4. Assure success by identifying, monitoring, and measuring results.

Sometimes a need gap is obvious. Homeless people need affordable, safe shelter; businesspeople desire freeways that aren't jammed every day at rush hour; and your customers may want new, less expensive technology that completely replaces what they are using. But sometimes the gap is not so obvious, and finding it requires exploring the current and desired situations.

1. Explore Needs and Goals

The main way to discover the need gap is by asking questions. Questioning is a very important skill. It makes persuasion easier by getting the person you want to influence involved in discovering the problem (where it "hurts") and being committed to creating the solution (how to make it feel "better").

"Judge a man by his questions rather than by his answers," Voltaire said. Indeed, well-phrased questions are the mark of a skilled persuader. Such queries help people organize their thoughts and feelings. Thus, you'll get tremendous insight into their needs, motivations, and fears. The answers will smooth the way for the building of a relationship.

Open versus Closed Questions – It's best to begin with open questions, the kind that require a narrative for an answer. Such questions can't be answered with a simple yes or no, or a simple fact. These open-ended questions encourage the other person to relax and to think broadly even as they give you a chance to explore.

Proper phrasing makes a big difference in the kind of answer you get. "How's business?" will often get you a pat answer. "Can you tell me a little bit about your business?" is a much better open question. Similarly, "Are you happy with your current mutual fund?" is not as good as "Would you describe your current personal investment strategy?" "Can you tell me what's important to you in a home-security system?" is likely to be more productive than "So, you want a burglar alarm?"

Open questions don't lead the other person in a specific direction but, rather, increase dialogue and show your interest in his or her situation. Once you've gathered information that paints a broad picture, you can use closed questions to get specific facts.

Let's suppose you're thinking about remodeling your home. The first contractor comes to your home and asks a few questions like: "How old is the home?" "What areas do you want to remodel?" "Will you need financing?"

"How much equity do you have in the house?" "When do you want the work to start?" Those are all reasonable closed questions that get the contractor some useful information.

Then a second contractor arrives and asks questions like: "Could you tell me a little about your lifestyle?" "Which area of your home is your favorite, and why?" "What do you hope to accomplish by getting this remodeling done?" Then, in addition, he asks the same questions the other contractor did.

Which contractor would you hire? My guess is, all other things being equal, you'd be more influenced by the second builder who started with the open questions, then went to the specific closed questions. He engaged you in an exploration of your need gap, your "because."

Or perhaps you're seeking donations to your university's alumni fund. A good open-ended question to a prospective donor might be: "How do you feel about being an alumna of State?" You can follow this with: "Are you aware of all the good work the alumni fund is doing?" Again, that's an open question followed by a closed question.

The Funnel Technique – The "funnel" technique of questioning involves beginning with broad, open questions and then building on those responses by making narrower, more specific queries. As you move down the neck of the funnel, you fill in more and more of the details by asking more pointed questions.

The broad, open questions at the top of the funnel ("What prompted you to look for a new travel agency right now?") are comfortable to answer and give the respondent more freedom. By the time you get to the more specific questions ("How many national trips and international trips, on the average, does your firm book in a month?"), he or she can see where you're going and will be more willing to share information with you. Not only that, most people will experience a higher sense of trust as they reveal information to you gradually.

Clarifying, Expanding, or Redirecting – It's also important to understand the three primary directions for questions: clarify, expand, or redirect. Clarifying questions refer directly to the other person's remarks. In essence, these questions suggest: I hear what you're saying but I want to make sure I know what you mean. Clarifying questions are a form of feedback, and they reinforce what the person just said.

70

Thus, the contractor might say: "Am I correct in thinking you hope to substantially cut down on your heating bills with this improvement?"

As a fund-raiser, you might ask: "You're saying that you're proud to be a university grad but you're not informed about what the alumni fund is doing these days?" By asking the person to repeat or affirm a statement, you're attempting to reinforce his or her need for your service or cause.

Expanding questions get at more detailed information, such as what the other person's priorities are. In essence, you're saying: I understand, but tell me more.

What if the contractor asked, "When this area is enlarged, what kind of furniture do you plan to put in here?" That would give him a better idea of your style preference. You might ask the prospective alumni-fund donor: "What kinds of activities were you involved in while you attended the university? What was your major?" Her answers might suggest a way to elicit her support.

Redirecting questions are useful for steering the conversation in other directions. In essence, you're saying: I now have a good grasp of your point of view, so let's look in another area. These questions can change the topic, or navigate a difficult exchange toward smoother waters. If the answer to an expanding question goes on and on, change the topic with a redirecting question.

A Collaborative Experience – Using questions makes persuasion more of a collaborative experience. Remember: increasing your persuasiveness is not an exercise in exerting power over people. Some folks may still cling to the old image of using verbal domination to get others to see things their way. But it doesn't work that way in the real world anymore, if it ever did.

Whether you're selling goods, recruiting people to work for political candidates, marshaling support for community causes, or trying to win over people for whatever reason, the emphasis now is on getting that person (1) to acknowledge and share a perceived need (again, a "because") and then (2) to be willing to collaborate with you on solutions.

You'll be a powerful persuader when you can align your vision with the needs, wants, and objectives of other people and get their feedback. Exploring those needs and getting the other person to acknowledge the need gap – the gap between what is and what can be, or the "because" – is the first crucial step.

2. Create and Select a Solution

Usually when you're trying to persuade somebody, there's more than one possible course of action. So in most cases, you'll want to involve the other person in exploring ways to close the need gap. If they're helping create the solution, they'll be far more committed to implementing it than if you unilaterally create the plan and "inflict" your solution on them. For instance, if you're a real-estate salesperson, you may find a great home that meets a family's living requirements. But it may not meet their criteria for quality of the schools or access to shopping. Or you may be able to meet all the requirements – including schools and shopping – but not at the right price. By collaborating with your customers, you can help solve the problem by getting them to detail their priorities, telling you which of the factors is most critical to their plan. That way, you'll help establish mutual respect and trust. Trust, says management author and speaker Gordon Shea, is the "miracle ingredient in organizational life – a lubricant that reduces friction, a bonding agent that glues together disparate parts, a catalyst that facilitates action."

The point is, you want to make others feel they have a part in the solution, not feel as if they were coerced or manipulated. Coercing someone into following your suggestions may get you what you want in the short term. But in the long term, you'll lose.

3. Commit to an Action Plan

If yours is a simple sale or other act of persuasion, if a yes or no is all that's required, action is immediate. But if what you're seeking requires several steps or phases, you'll need agreement on how you're going to proceed.

Doctors, for example, often complain that patients don't get well because they don't fully follow the prescription directions. When the patient starts feeling a little better, for example, he or she may stop taking the medicine. Even though the doctor is in charge of the treatment, the patient acts unilaterally and then the doctor gets blamed for the relapse.

Maybe the doctor needs to take time to explain the action of the drugs in relation to the problem. The symptoms of a sore throat can be alleviated in two days with an antibiotic, the physician might say, but the germs may remain for days afterward, and they need to be controlled. Patients who understand the process are much more likely to carry out the plan.

During this step, make sure the other person clearly understands the benefits of implementation. Have them restate the benefits and what it's going to take to get them. For instance, the contractor might encourage the customer to say, "If I invest $10,000 in this remodeling plan now, my house will be worth more when it comes time to sell it, and I'll also save between $500 and $700 a year in heating costs."

An added plus of discussing the follow-up may be that the customer comes up with benefits that the salesperson never thought of. "If I remodel, I can also use the added space for a home office, meaning I no longer will need to rent space downtown and I may be able to take an added deduction on my income taxes."

Politics. When you hit the "politics" barrier, it means that agreement will put somebody at odds with somebody else: "If I buy that new car, my wife will kill me." "If I join one more save-the-environment organization, my husband will move my things out into the garden."

Because you're committed to collaboration, you won't ignore such a concern or suggest that it just be ignored. Instead, find out why that third person feels that way. Maybe you can alleviate the concern with new information. You might say to the prospective car buyer, "Why don't you bring your wife down here on Saturday for a test drive, and we can see what her specific concerns are." To the prospective organization member, you could add, "Here's what we do that's different from all the other environmental groups. Do you think your husband would be supportive of that?" In a situation where agreement is blocked by politics, all you can do is help to create solutions.

Postponement. When the other person says, "I need time to think about it," it's very important to find out the real reason for postponement. It can simply be a polite way of saying no. It could be that the person never makes hasty decisions. Or the person may not have all the information he needs and is too embarrassed or too timid to ask for more.

This is where clarifying questions come in handy. "Is anything confusing to you?" "What specifically can I do to help the process along?" "Will you be comparing my offer with someone else's?" Asking questions keeps the door open for agreement.

At the root of this postponement may be personal discomfort. Something about what you're suggesting makes the other person uncomfortable. Maybe they can't even put their finger on it. But chances are their discomfort has to do with risk. You need to find out what they see as the risk.

One technique is to have them list the pros and cons from their point of view. If your suggestion costs money, you can offer a money-back guarantee. If it's membership in an organization, invite them to a meeting with absolutely no pressure to join. If they're put off by a product's unfamiliarity, invite them to try it out.

Provide whatever information you can to give the other person confidence in what you're offering. You can even help them identify the key factors they should take into account before agreeing with you. You can also alleviate personal discomfort and postponement by showing – and this is very important! – that the benefit far outweighs the risk. So remember to explain clearly the WIIFM factor, or "What's In It For Me?"

Personality Conflict. Even if what you're suggesting or offering seems positive to the other person, he/she may not like you. The relationship between the two of you is the foundation of the persuasion process. If that relationship collapses, so does everything it supports.

One of the most common causes of a personality conflict is a breakdown in trust. Maybe what you were offering really didn't have the other person's interest at heart. Or you made promises you didn't keep. Or something went wrong, and you made no attempt to address the problem. At other times, the personality conflict is simply the result of different styles of communicating.

Priorities. The other person may think that your idea, product, or cause is a good one, but it's not among his/her top ten priorities. This is when knowing yourself well is very important. The better you can articulate why you value what you're advocating (the "because" factor again), the better your chances of striking a chord with the other person.

When trying to persuade others, you might need to help them articulate what their priorities are – in other words, what they value most. The exploring phase we talked about earlier is the perfect time to investigate the other person's priorities. Then you can emphasize both the intrinsic value of the idea, product, or cause as well as how it serves the person's priorities.

4. Assure Success by Identifying, Monitoring, and Measuring Results

In California's Silicon Valley, where many of America's most technologically advanced firms compete fiercely, there's an adage: you can't manage what you can't measure. Things change so fast in that high-tech arena, those computer executives say, that it's absolutely critical to get your hands on the numbers and to do so quickly.

There's a lesson in that for the rest of us. While the real secret to long-term influence and power with people is exceeding their expectations, they often don't have a firm idea of what they expect. So you need to help them, first, identify criteria for success. As much as possible, put those goals in quantitative terms – return on investment, say, or number of years a product should last, or the maximum amount of maintenance needed. Offer them something concrete.

Second, you need to help them manage their expectations. If they expect too much, you'll fail; if the expectations are too low, anybody could match them. So the secret is helping the person you're influencing try to come up with realistic quantitative expectations.

Finally, you need to measure the promised results and be available if a problem develops. You've got to keep an eye on the results and consult with the other person about how he or she sees them.

What happens if the room addition your company built develops leaks during the first rainy season? What do you do if the elderly woman you recruited to save the trees in the park gets put in jail for joining a protest? In either case, you need to be there, be supportive, and do what's needed to correct the situation.

In other words, the real work of persuading people and maintaining influence with people occurs after they say yes. Staying in touch with the people you want to influence, and staying tuned in to their values and needs, are what this fourth stage is all about.

———————•••———————

As the DVD presentation shut off, Jack was finishing his dessert of his favorite ice cream "Extreme Moose Tracks." He pulled out his sales journal and began to write.

My Takeaways on *Becoming More Persuasive* by Dr. Tony Alessandra

1. Remember, we are all persuaders. We do it every day.
2. Four-step persuasion process:
   a. Explore my clients' needs and goals
   b. Create and select a solution to their challenges
   c. Commit to an action plan
   d. Assure success by identifying, monitoring, and measuring my results
3. Questions open doors. Using questions makes persuasion more of a collaborative experience for all involved.
4. Have clients list the pros and cons from their point of view when they push off taking action.

Chapter Six

Instant Rapport Building

The Psychology of Exceptional Customer Connections
By Dr. Larry Iverson

"Charge!" yelled the crowd. As the organ at Great American Ballpark in downtown Cincinnati continued to excite the crowd, Jack and Digger sat eating hotdogs in their box seats. They were as excited as everyone else in the stadium. Who knows where Digger got the box seats? He wouldn't say. He had just called Jack at mid-day and said, "After work, grab your Reds hat. I got us tickets to the 7:10 PM game versus the Dodgers." He had said nothing about box seats. Jack had expected them to turn upward towards the stairs to the upper deck when Digger had turned to the left towards the field.

"Two down, score tied at two a piece here in the bottom of the 8th inning on a balmy summer evening here in downtown Cincinnati," said Digger. He loved to give the play by play as if he were the Reds Hall of Famer announcer Marty Brennaman. "Here comes Joey Votto, the Reds all-star first baseman. Man on second and a base hit from Votto would put the Reds on top. The pitch, it's a hard line drive into the corner in right field. Run scores and Votto on his way to second with a stand up double."

At the beginning of the game, it had been hard for Jack to get used to this play-by-play action from his seat companion. But, as the game progressed, he began to appreciate the child-like enthusiasm from this sales genius sitting beside him.

As they were driving home after enjoying a four to three Reds victory, Digger said, "Sales champions are made the same way baseball champions are made. In fact, even more so. It takes a lot of hard work and study at your craft. I am proud of you, Jack. You have worked very hard these last few months and now you are showing a lot of fruit. You have not only become one of the best in your company, but you are on your way to becoming one of the all-stars in your industry. Just like Joey Votto, once you reach the top, you have to continue to work hard to stay there, sometimes even harder. There is no coasting in the world of selling."

"I have another article for you to read. It is from Larry Iverson. It is all about rapport and connecting with your clients. As you know Jack, without rapport there is no sale."

I want to welcome you to Instant Rapport Building, The Psychology of Exceptional Customer Connections. Would knowing what communications promote good will and what communications turn customers off be a benefit to you? Have you ever lost a customer and wondered how to bring him/her back? Would knowing what drives and motivates customers to take immediate action help you out?

Well, starting today, you can apply strategies that boost your customers' connection to you. We're now going to look at proven methods for improving your communication and eliminating loyalty barriers between you and your customer. We're going to look at how to read non-verbal communications more accurately and more easily.

You're going to understand the drivers that stimulate loyalty. You're going to know how to build rapport quickly so potential customers want to work with you. You'll also learn how to overcome negatives and trigger a positive mindset rapidly and learn the keys to creating a positive customer mindset about you, your organization, and your products.

Churchill on Self-Leadership

World War II had ended, the treaties had been signed, and Winston Churchill was being interviewed by dozens of journalists asking him why the allied powers won the war and what made the difference? How come the axis powers didn't come out on top?

Mr. Churchill talked about numerous things that stood out and made a difference, but the one thing he said mattered more than anything else was what he called "individual leadership." He said both sides had great generals. Both had good armies. They had amazing weapons, and in some ways, the axis powers even had weapons that surpassed the allies. But he said the real difference was the war effort.

People at home were really making a difference. They were doing what they could to make sure the troops knew they were supported. Take the post office, for instance. In many cases, if you had a letter to send but didn't have enough postage to mail it to someone overseas, they would send it without postage. Why? Because it was that important to make sure the people over there knew you were thinking about them.

There was music being played continuously on the armed forces radio network overseas, so troops could hear music from home, reminding them of why they were there fighting.

And Mr. Churchill talked about self-leadership and what made the difference in this individual initiative. He made a statement that he became famous for. This applies as we begin to talk about creating a connection between us and our customers.

Mr. Churchill said, "To every person there comes a time in life, that special moment when they're figuratively tapped on the shoulder and offered the chance to do a very special thing, unique to them and fitted to his or her talent. What a tragedy if that moment finds them unprepared or unqualified for the work which would be their finest hour!"

This comment says many things. First, it doesn't say that just the people at the very top of the hierarchy are the only ones who can make a difference. It says, "...to every person there comes a time in life...." It also says that each of us has something to offer. Each of us has unique skills we can do. And, we need to be ready.

With sales and customer service, you need to be ready. You need to be ready for whatever comes down the road at you. This may include customers' problems or organizational issues that get in the way. So we need to be ready. We need to learn. We need to grow, and we need to be self-led.

Task vs. Relationship in Sales and Service

Have you ever gone out to dinner at a really nice restaurant? Have you also eaten at a fast food restaurant of some sort?

Is there a difference in the quality of service and the type of food you get between the high-end five-star restaurants and the fast food restaurant? You can bet there is.

Now both of them are acceptable. When you go to the nice restaurant, you have certain expectations for the type of food you're going to receive, how much you'll pay there, and the type of service you'll receive. When you go to the fast food restaurant, you have different expectations for how they're going to treat you, the type of food you'll get, and how much you'll pay.

The Contrast in Service & Task/Product

Let's say that you go out with your significant other or with a good friend to a really nice dinner at one of the finest restaurants where you live. When you get there, you're seated immediately. It's beautiful, the ambiance is wonderful, and the aromas are great. Let's say that the food there is truly spectacular, and not only that, but you also find out that this night everything on the menu is 50% off as a customer appreciation gesture. So, you order and wait expectantly to have this amazing food. And it does get served finally, but it takes them four and a half hours to get your dinner on the table! Is that okay?! I don't think so!!!

Let's change this scenario. Imagine that this exceptional restaurant you go to has amazing service. There's actually someone dedicated to your table alone. If you take a drink of water, they automatically pour you more water. If you take a bite of your roll, they instantly serve you another. Whatever you want, the service is just stunning, actually it's spectacular—but the food is so bad that you can barely gag it down! Is that all right? No, of course not.

We need both a good product and decent service. You want reasonable food at a decent price, and you want to be treated a certain way in the process. Selling and Service go hand in hand.

You As A Provider

Let's look at the two components in the way you do business. Let's say that you are the best at your job, ever in the history of your field. There has never been anyone better than you. If there were a gold medal given like they do in the Olympics, you would easily win it.

Actually, 50 years from now, people will look back and say, "You should have seen them 50 years ago! They were just amazing! The service they gave was just incredible." So you are amazing at doing the task—but you are such an obnoxious, mean, nasty sucker that nobody can stand you! Everybody detests you! Do you think your job is going to go well, even if you have the best product there is? Not even....

Let's say, on the other hand, that you are very warm, loving, and kind to your customers and co-workers. Everybody just adores you. You are so sweet—people just follow you around at work. They want to even be in your shadow, just to feel your presence, because you are so wonderful. But—at the same time, you don't have a brain in your head! You couldn't do the job if you had to! You have no product knowledge and no skills whatsoever. Is that going to work? Probably not—even if you are the nicest person in your organization.

You need them both. You need to be able to do the job in an intelligent, straightforward fashion, and you need to be able to deal effectively with human beings you encounter.

So let's begin to look at what you can do to greatly enhance your quality of sales and customer service.

Proprietary Interest

Are you self-employed? Yes, you are.

Whether you work for yourself, a large corporation, or a government agency, you are self-employed and every day you are selling you. You are running your own business.

There's a business principle that says those organizations that have the greatest growth, that move forward and keep growing, do so because each person inside that organization takes a 'proprietary interest' in the business.

Proprietary interest means you act as if you are the proprietor—the owner. It's your business. You are the one who runs it. You're the person who takes care of it. A proprietary interest means you are self-employed. You are the business, and your territories, your customers, the people you work with, are central to your success as a business.

The Seven Principles of Partnering

There are seven principles crucial to successful partnering. These principles have been found to be deeply embedded within organizations that thrive and grow.

1. The Principle of Relationships

The first of the seven principles is the principle of relationships. Success in partnering is directly determined by your ability to establish and maintain rapport with customers.

Creating a quality relationship is essential. Your customer will not collaborate with you long term unless they believe you are acting in his or her best interest. The higher the level of trust between you and your customer, the lower will be their resistance that gets generated by fear of making a mistake, acceptance of your suggestions.

Why do people have problems with letting go of their fears? Why do people resist? Because of history, time, and past performance. They want to understand what's going to happen, how it's going to happen, when it's going to happen, and where it's going to happen. So, we must build our relationships.

It's like cooking a meal. The relationship takes a little bit of time to simmer. So, you have to take the time to grow the relationship.

2. The Principle of Sales

Nothing in life occurs unless a sale has taken place—nothing.

Everyone likes to buy, but no one likes to be pressured or hard-sold. The top salespeople are viewed by their customers as servers who help them get what they need or want. You are self-employed and are responsible for the success of your business.

The word 'sales' comes from an Old English word, "Selje," which means 'to serve'.

If you think about it, the most effective salespeople, the best customer servers, truly serve their way into great relationships and to assisting customers to get what they want or need.

The principle of sales says we are always selling. Every day you had better sell your boss on keeping you, versus firing you and hiring someone else. You had better sell other employees on working with you and collaborating, versus sabotaging you.

If you have customers, you need to be selling them on the benefits of working with you and partnering with you. If you're in a relationship, you had better be selling your partner every single day, because if you don't, there will come a day when he/she will go find someone who is prettier, handsomer, funnier, richer, more entertaining, better skill sets, etc. You'd better be selling your partner every day that you're the best package around.

The principle of sales applies everywhere.

3. The Principle of Goals

To achieve your dreams, you must have clearly defined, written goals that you believe are attainable.

The success you create is in direct proportion to your level of desire and your sustained vision and commitment to becoming the best you can be.

Written goals assist in keeping you on course when the winds of life try and blow you in the wrong direction. We need to find a way to make certain we stay on track. Goals are the way to do it.

It's been discovered that 94% of those individuals, who are in the top 3% of the most successful, have clearly defined written goals. To assist yourself in getting where you want to go, you need to have clearly defined goals. As a psychologist, I've also found that those individuals who live longer, healthier, more fulfilling lives have goals.

Humans as a species have a tendency to have their health diminish when they no longer have a reason to live. Having goals gives you that reason to be alive—to be, to do, and to interact. The principle of goals assists you in staying on track and is vitally important to your success.

4. The Principle of Need

The decision to work with a partner is a result of an attempt to satisfy a need or to overcome dissatisfaction.

Before beginning a project with anyone, you need to be really clear about the need you're attempting to satisfy. Talking alone will not uncover needs. Only by asking clear, specific, targeted questions will the answers be forthcoming.

Years ago while visiting a friend in his office, I noticed that one of his walls was covered with postcards, plaques, sayings, and little banners. While he was gone to a meeting for few minutes, I read a number of these sayings on his walls.

One of them applies to the principle of need. It said, "Every morning in Africa a gazelle wakes up and knows it must run faster than the fastest lion. A lion wakes up every morning and knows it must outrun the slowest gazelle or it will starve to death. It doesn't matter if you are a lion or a gazelle—when the sun comes up, you'd better be running."

That is the principle of need in action. You've got to be in motion and making progress. You have to be moving forward. So, applying the Principle of Need to helping your customers get what they want is beneficial to you and to them.

5. The Principle of Influence

In every relationship, one person is more influential than the other. In partnerships, the influence is quite often passed back and forth between partners.

If you are more influential, they accept your input and recommendations. If they are more influential, you accept their perspective or methods.

People seek to satisfy the greatest number of unmet needs, the easiest way, in the most expedient manner. To do that, they must first influence themselves to take action, and secondly, influence others to participate in achieving the results.

Influence is in the midst of every relationship you participate in. Not just customer service relationships at work, but also your relationships at home, people who participate in hobbies you may have, interactive groups you are involved with in the community, your church, and so on and so on.

The ability to influence makes a major difference. Your skills at persuading and having influence in many cases will determine your success at attaining the goals you have before you.

6. The Principle of Preparation

The best customer servers prepare thoroughly prior to each contact, and they debrief their results afterwards.

Customers are looking for solutions. Sales and customer service champions plan questions in advance, thereby assisting customers to focus more easily, clearly, and quickly on solutions.

To feel most confident and perform at your peak requires putting the needed time into the preparation. The principle of preparation sets you up to be a success. Spending time thinking about where you're going, what you want to achieve, perhaps writing an agenda for a meeting you'll be involved in, takes the time. But—it's time well spent.

It's rare that I go to any meeting without preparing an agenda. Even if the other party says they'll have one, I take one with me. At least 70% of the meetings I go to, the other person or organization has not done one.

Even if they do have an agenda, if we get through theirs, I can throw mine on the table and say, "Here are a few more things I'd like to clarify." And if they don't have any written agenda, then I really am in control of the meeting. I can take it into the area most important to me.

Being prepared, being ready to have that important conversation, can make a gigantic difference for you.

7. The Principle of Perspective

The best business people are viewed by their customers as a consultant, an adviser or a partner, not as a sales person. You'll achieve great results through educating your customers into how your business works and how to satisfy their needs. The Principle of Perspective says it is vital to understand the other person's perspective, because there is a great chance that the way they see things is not perfectly aligned with your point-of-view.

Here's a little story about perspective. This is a letter written home from an 18-year-old freshman daughter at college, to her mother and father.

Dear Mom and Dad,

I don't know if you heard about this on the news a couple of months ago, but my dorm burned down. I didn't want to worry you, so I went out on my own and found a place to live. It's even cheaper than the dorm was. It's really a great deal. Not only that, but I can cook my own food, which is much better than dorm food. It's a beautiful Victorian house close to campus.

There are eight of us living there, and one of my roommates is an extremely talented musician. He's the most youthful 40-year-old person I have ever met.

Well, he and I fell in love. I couldn't believe it—we just have a magical connection. I never thought it would happen to me, but it has. I've now moved into his room, so we can save money by not having to pay for two rooms.

I also made a decision not too long ago, to help him further his musical career. I'm going to quit school so I can go to work and support him. I just know he's going to be a big star one day, and I can help take care of him until he makes it big.

The other day, I wasn't feeling very well so he suggested I go to the doctor and I did. Guess what, the doctor said I'm pregnant!

Now, Mom and Dad I want you to know I'm not really pregnant. And, I'm really feeling just fine. No, I've not fallen in love with a 40-year-old man and moved in with him. I'm still living in my dorm; it did not burn down. I'm actually quite happy with the way things are going in my life right now.

So, Mom and Dad, if you think about how bad things could be—is getting a C minus in English, and a D in Chemistry, really that big of a deal?

Love, Suzie

Now that's perspective.........

Take the time to begin applying the seven principles of partnering: Incorporate the principles of relationships, of sales, goals, need, influence, preparation, and perspective. You will begin more effectively growing connections between you and your customers that will last a lifetime.

Customer loyalty is built over time, and the better you build the relationships, sell effectively, and have targeted goals, the more likely it is that your customers are going to be happy, satisfied, and want to work with you long term. Using these seven principles of successful partnering can make a significant difference to you and your business.

———————•••• •———————

After he had read the inspiring article, Jack noticed that Digger had scribbled some thoughts on the back of it. He began to read...

Digger Jones' Power Nuggets from Larry Iverson's article

1. Remember the wise words of Winston Churchill when he said, "To every person there comes a time in life, that special moment when they're figuratively tapped on the shoulder and offered the chance to do a very special thing, unique to them and fitted to his or her talent. What a tragedy if that moment finds them unprepared or unqualified for the work which would be their finest hour!" *This is your time! Grab hold of it...work hard...believe...and make it happen!*
2. Successful Selling and Great Customer Service go hand in hand. They are opposite sides of the same coin.
3. You are self-employed.
4. "The higher the level of trust between you and your customer, the lower will be their resistance that gets generated by fear of making a mistake, acceptance of your suggestions." Larry Iverson
5. "Nothing in life occurs unless a sale has taken place—nothing." Larry Iverson
6. Top salespeople are "servers to their clients." The root word in which our word "sales" comes from is the Old English word "selje," which is defined as "to serve."

7. Motion is momentum. To succeed, you must take action…every day!
8. Prepare, Prepare, Prepare!
9. You are a consultant.

Chapter Seven

Disciplined Selling Makes Sales Champions

By Mark Bowser

At 6:00 AM, Jack's "opportunity clock," as Zig Ziglar would put it, sounded off announcing the new day. Jack stretched and climbed out of bed. He opened the blinds to his bedroom and was greeted with a bright sunshiny new day. Jack walked to the door of his apartment and opened it to grab his Cincinnati Enquirer. He sat down at his kitchen and opened it to what had become his favorite column *The Business Edge* by Mark Bowser.

"Well, let's see what tools Mr. Bowser has for us today," said Jack to himself. "Hmmm, great title." Jack began to read.

———————•●●•———————

Have you ever attempted to coach first and second grade boys' basketball? It is a lot like herding cats. I am enjoying the experience of helping coach my son Andrew's Upward Basketball team. We are known as the Minutemen. I have learned a great deal through this experience. A great deal about discipline. Why? Because starting out, we had none. We only have one game left in our season...and we still have very little discipline.

It is amazing. As coaches, we will tell them one thing in the huddle, and in less than two minutes, it has seeped out of their brains and they are performing on pure emotion running up and down the court like a bunch of hyenas who just ate a chocolate bar full of sugar. Sometimes, I feel that they have the memory of a gnat.

Now, part of that is about being a young boy, but if this energy isn't harnessed, it could mean disaster down the road for their lives. Even though they have been very successful from a scoreboard perspective, we as coaches believed it was vital to put in place a focused, mandatory, disciplined set of rules.

Since the day we implemented our disciplined rules of engagement, we have seen a marked improvement in their behavior, communication, and future success. I say future success because discipline doesn't always create immediate success on the basketball court...or on the court of life. But, we believe it is imperative to shape these boys for lifetime success, not just immediate, temporary success.

The same is true with your career in the world of selling. Undisciplined sales professionals have starving wallets. So, today I have for you a game plan for disciplined selling. If acted upon consistently, I am convinced you will see future success. Again, there is that word "future." We don't like the word "future." We much prefer the word "now." Unfortunately, the word "now" is all about comfort. The true champions of sales, and basketball, put aside the comfort of now and focus on the habits of now that create the success of the future.

The first element of our disciplined selling is that of Commitment. Commitment is success. It was Andrew Carnegie who said, "The average person puts only 25% of his energy and ability into his work. The world takes off its hat to those who put in more than 50% of their capacity, and stands on its head for those few and far between souls who devote 100%." You have to make a decision right now before you read another word. Okay, read these next couple of sentences and then stop and make your decision. Are you committed to this career path called selling? Are you committed to the company you work for? Are you committed and passionate about your product or service? If you can't answer all of those questions with a resounding "yes," then stop reading right now and figure out what you can say "yes" to.

The second element in our game plan of disciplined selling is to be an Early Riser. Yes, I hate it too, but the verdict is out. The ones who are successful are usually the ones who are up first, many times even before the sun gets out of bed. As I began writing this article this morning, it was dark outside. The kids were still in bed, and my wife was in the bathroom getting dressed. Tomorrow morning, set your alarm clock for...early. Form this habit and much of the rest will take care of itself.

The third element is to Read & Listen to books and audiobooks on Sales Success. In fact, early in the morning is a great time to do this. Hey, you are going to be up anyway.

Research shows that if you read (or listen) to just one sales book a month, that in five years you will be in the top 5% of sales professionals in the world in terms of selling knowledge. Now, knowledge is not enough. We have all heard that "knowledge is power." That is a bunch of garbage. Knowledge will give you nothing but frustration unless you take action on it. That is the key. Put into action the selling philosophies and strategies that you learn during your reading and listening.

Fourth: Toughness. Toughness is a word that is used a great deal in sports. But what is toughness when it comes to selling? Toughness is doing the things that you don't want to do. Toughness is forcing yourself out of bed early or reading books like we have already mentioned...even when you don't want to. Toughness is scheduling one more appointment for the day when you would prefer to head home or to the tennis court. In a nutshell, toughness is doing the things that the average salesperson isn't willing to do so that you can create a future where you can do what you want to do.

And, our fifth and last element for disciplined selling is Continual Prospecting & Setting Appointments. I don't care how good you are, if you don't have anyone to sell to, then you aren't going to be successful. Many sales professionals hate to prospect, but it is arguably the most important part of the sales process. Get on a disciplined schedule of setting appointments. I am going to go out on a limb here. If you will double your time in front of people who can buy...you might just double your income. Isn't this clever stuff?

———————•••••———————

"Good stuff today, Mark." Jack said to the column as if the author were sitting in the same room with him. Jack remembered not too long ago the lousy discipline he had as a salesperson. On most days, he wouldn't see the other side of his pillow until 8:30 AM. Lately, things had been different. A small smile creased the corners of Jack's mouth.

Chapter Eight

Top 7 Personality Challenges

By Dawn Jones

J ack entered the Montgomery Inn Boathouse BBQ Restaurant on the Cincinnati side of the Ohio River. It was 11:56 AM, and his weekly Sales Master Mind Club meeting was to start at noon on the dot. Just enough time to hit the restroom before heading up to the meeting. He had been looking forward to this meeting for weeks. For one, the food was going to be awesome. The Master Mind Group met at a different restaurant every week. But two, Jack was looking forward to this meeting. They had a guest speaker today to kick off the meeting. Her name was Dawn Jones. Jack had never met her but had heard some good stuff about her. She recently had an audio program go orbital in sales on iTunes.

There was a wonderful buffet, and Jack chose the half rack of pork BBQ ribs, corn on the cob, and their famous Saratoga chips. He sat down and began to catch up on the week's happenings with his sales buddies. About fifteen minutes into the meal, their club president introduced Dawn Jones and she began to speak...and what a presentation it was.

———————•●●•———————

Good afternoon. It is good to spend this time with you. Thanks for inviting me. When it comes to answering the question, what is success, a key component is how effectively you communicate with people who are different than you. During our time together, we will explore the Top 7 Personality Challenges along with the secrets for successful communication with those differing personality types.

So let me ask you a question. When you think about communicating with success, what does that look like to you? Do you picture someone who can capture the attention of any audience, then clearly communicate their thoughts and ideas while motivating people to action? Perhaps you see someone confidently connecting with people regardless of personality, position, or title, even despite their age or gender, irrespective of culture or generation. Perhaps you envision someone who comfortably talks with everyone; be it large groups or individually one-on-one. Whether you are a CEO or VP of a Fortune 500 company or the CEO or VP of your home, regardless of what industry you are in or what position you hold, the power to communicate with success is not only possible but is within your grasp because together for the next few minutes, we will discuss the tips, techniques, and tools of making communicating with success a reality starting right now.

During our time together, we will explore how you can live your life with all people in a way that will allow you to recognize the type of personality the person you are speaking with has along with the discernment to recognize which personality challenge you are facing and the techniques to successfully communicate with that personality type. My desire is to help you gain confidence while making successful communication conceivable in all areas of your life. I care about you and your time. Now, even though I don't know you, I know that you want something out of this presentation and I look forward to helping you become the best communicator possible. So let's jump in.

I tie this concept into something I learned from Steven Covey's 7 Habits of Highly Effective People, habit #2: begin with the end in mind. I start just about every seminar, training, and coaching session with this concept because the clearer your target the better chance you will have of hitting it, and the more you know about what motivates the people you are speaking with the more you can weave what is important to them into your target.

Think about what areas of communication you would like to target and improve upon as I list out the areas we will cover together today beginning with identifying your communication style and knowing how well you put your personality type to work for you. Do you recognize the strengths along with the cautions of your personality style? Or would you like to get better at recognizing those differences and putting them to work for you? Or how about knowing when and how to successfully shift gears when communicating with someone who is different than you without seeming overbearing, weak, or fake. There are four personalities to choose from; are you choosing the right one? Part of your communication style is your personality. During this next section, we'll explore how well you are putting your personality to work for you as well as when to shift gears.

You may have taken a personality test at some point in your life, such as the Myers-Briggs or the DISK, or even one based on numbers or colors. Some tests are based on science and research while others are purely entertaining. Now there are some inaccuracies when a person is testing himself/herself, which is referred to as self-reporting, rather than being tested by a neutral observer. Wikipedia Encyclopedia puts it this way: "one problem with self-report measures of personality is that respondents are often able to distort their responses. This is particularly problematic in employment contexts and other contexts where important decisions are being made and there is an incentive to present oneself in a favorable manner." Here is why this is important: these tests can be skewed by our own bias, but reactions can't be and here is what I mean. A person can answer based on what they think the person giving the test might be looking for whereas a person will reveal their personality and character when they react to circumstances they encounter, especially if they are under pressure.

I like to put it this way: you can tell a lot about a person's personality by the way they react in pressure situations such as if their luggage gets lost, or if they get lost, or if things don't go their way. This is what I call "character under fire," and try as we might, we can't fake or skew those scores. What we demonstrate in those pressure situations reveals who we are and gives a snapshot of our personality. Though there are several things to factor in to people's reactions, including temperament, upbringing, social norms, and practiced behaviors, personality is a big part of this equation.

For our time together, we are going to focus on four basic personalities. These are the same four that Socrates referred to back around 450 or 400 years before Christ, and scientists agree that your character is a mix of these four basic personality types. To bring in a modern day translation, I've renamed the four different personality styles and I will refer to them as the direct person, the thinker/analyzer, the social extrovert, and the relational person. As I list out each style, I will also include the following 7 challenges along with solutions so that we can communicate with success regardless of any personality challenge we face.

The first challenge we will cover is recognizing which personality type or blend of personality types you are communicating with. With this challenge, I will point out the key expressions or phrases that different personality types use so you can quickly recognize the personality and overcome the challenge you are facing by speaking in a similar fashion.

With challenge #2, I will walk you through understanding the self-esteem level of the different personality styles. To help you overcome this challenge, I will also give you self-esteem motivators for each personality. With challenge #3, I will give you the cautions to be aware of with each personality style. In challenge #4, I will include the types of vocations best suited for each personality style along with some cautions if a certain personality style is in the wrong job. For challenge #5, I'll list out the main areas of improvement for each personality style. During challenge #6, we will go over conversations or actions that irritate or annoy the different personality styles. And for challenge #7, I'll give you the best way to communicate with each personality style including how to adjust your tone, tempo, and body language so that your words can impact the direction of the conversation to ensure you are communicating with success.

The first aspect I want to cover regarding your personality style is whether your style is based more on logic or emotions. Here is a quick way to tell. Direct people and thinker/analyzers tend to be more logical in their reactions whereas social extroverts and relational tend to be more emotional in their reactions. As I list out the specific characteristics of each personality, write down or take a mental note of which ones best describe you.

The Direct Person

Challenge 1: Personality of the Direct Person

Let's begin with the direct person. Direct people are direct, bottom line, and to the point. They are natural leaders and quick decision makers who tend to be vocal and say what is on their mind. Because they base their decisions mostly on logic, not emotions, sometimes they can come across as harsh, abrasive, or insensitive to people who are not direct. Some expressions of direct people are, "it's nothing personal; it's just business," or they might say, "get thicker skin," or "don't take things so personally," or they might tell you to get to the point. Direct people are competitive and want to be the best. As a result, they often times will tell you what you are doing wrong and they are hard pressed to hand out compliments as they expect you to do an excellent job, and if you are not doing that, you'll hear about it. Because of their leadership skills and decision-making abilities, they get things done, though they might ruffle a few feathers in the process.

Challenge 2: Understanding Self-Esteem/Expressions of the Direct Person

Direct people draw a lot of their self-esteem from being the best, achieving something that has never been accomplished before, and taking risks.

Challenge 3: Cautions of Communicating with the Direct Person

Some cautions are direct people will move to the "do it" part of the project, sometimes without fully defining or planning what the "do it" part is, which can leave team members, colleagues, and friends frustrated because they are the ones who often get blamed for the failure of a project or event when the reality could be that friends, colleagues, and team members might be afraid to speak up or say something to the direct person for fear of a very vocal and public reprimand.

Challenge 4: Vocations for the Direct Person

Some vocations that direct people are drawn to include supervisory or management positions, athletic or competitive vocations, or anything where they can compete to be the best and/or tell people what to do. They can also be drawn to law enforcement and firefighting. You will also find direct people at C-level positions, you know, CEO, CFO, CIO, though these executive positions are usually given to direct people who have learned to reign in this dominant style and blend it with the other ones. Bottom line with the direct people, from a very young age, they have been taking risks and telling people what to do and now they get paid for it.

Challenge 5: Areas to Improve for the Direct Person

Some areas to improve: listening skills, yes, even if it hurts. Listening and hearing and then repeating what the other person is saying before responding or reacting. Now, I know this may seem redundant to a direct person, but just saying "I get it" or "I hear you" is not enough as the other personality styles need to hear you repeat their words back to them. Also, when speaking in a disagreement, watch your volume, keep it to a speaking level or inside voice, watch your tone, keep it neutral, not condescending, and watch your intensity. Not everything is a fire, so you don't have to show up to every discussion with a fire hose! Often times, a drinking straw will suffice.

Challenge 6: Irritants and Annoyances to the Direct Person

Now here are some conversations or actions that irritate or annoy direct people: ones with too many details or conversations that jump around in a random manner or projects where plans are constantly changing and people who drag their feet when making decisions.

Challenge 7: How to Communicate with the Direct Person

The best way to communicate with direct people: be brief, be brilliant, be-gone! Don't be redundant and don't be-labor the point. As for tone, tempo, and body language lean towards a more assertive almost aggressive tone. Speak at a fast rate and be confident in your stance and body language with intentional and purposeful moves. Now if you are a direct person, you might be thinking to yourself, "Okay, got my part, let's move on." Now here is where I am going to bring in the other three styles into this equation because, as I said earlier, when you have the ability to reign in your style and learn how to communicate with the other three styles, that's when you'll start seeing the results and communicating with success. With that in mind, let's move now to thinkers/analyzers.

The Thinker / Analyzer

Challenge 1: Personality of the Thinker/Analyzer

Thinkers/analyzers are also logical in their approach, but unlike direct people, they love details. They are natural planners. In fact, I like to say that thinkers/analyzers are born with drop down menus in their head. They have a plan A, a plan B, a plan C, and a backup plan, just in case. Rather than being vocal, they tend to process their thoughts internally while considering all their options. As a result, they are more cautious and methodical in their decision making, which also takes a bit more time. They are constantly looking at the how and the why of situations or projects. How does this work? How much time do we have? How much will this cost? Why are we doing it this way? Thinkers/analyzers love breaking down projects into processes, and if graphs and charts are involved, even better.

Challenge 2: Understanding Self-Esteem/Expressions of the Thinker/ Analyzer

Some expressions of thinkers/analyzers: "if you are going to do it, then do it right" or "there is a place for everything and everything has its place" or "lack of planning on your part does not mean emergency on my part," though this one they don't often say out loud; they usually think it to themselves. They draw a lot of their self-esteem and personal value from being considered intelligent, precise, and accurate.

Challenge 3: Cautions of Communicating with the Thinker/Analyzer

Some cautions are because thinkers/analyzers are constantly breaking things down into minute details, and sometimes they can become paralyzed in thought and struggle with decision making, also known as analysis paralysis if they think they don't have all of the information to make a decision. Thinkers/analyzers also tend to be perfectionists and can be very harsh on themselves as well as with others if they don't do it right. For example, they would rather re-write an entire form rather than cross something out or use white-out as they hate mistakes. Thinkers/analyzers tend not to express themselves when they are frustrated or stuck. Instead, they keep it inside and go over and over the issue in their minds, either remaining stuck with the problem or when mastering that personality style, moving towards solutions.

Challenge 4: Vocations for the Thinker/Analyzer

Types of vocations thinkers/analyzers are drawn to include engineering, bookkeeping, IT, analysts, CPAs, computer programming, and even project managing if they have enough directness in them along with some good people skills, and possibly architecture if they have enough social extrovert in them.

Challenge 5: Areas to Improve for the Thinker/Analyzer

Some areas to improve on include decision-making and developing people skills. If you are a thinker/analyzer, give yourself permission to make decisions that aren't critical without exploring every option. For example, a simple one you can implement right away: next time you go to lunch, make your decision on the first thing you see that you would like to order off the menu rather than reading the entire menu two or three times. Give yourself permission to do your best rather than striving for perfectionism. Try a few little things like crossing something out on a form and finally, practice improving your people skills, practice being vocal, things such as small talk and mingling. Tell people what you are thinking without overwhelming them with all the details, think "top 3 bullet points," and put your problem solving skills to work by focusing on solutions not just problems.

Challenge 6: Irritants and Annoyances to the Thinker/ Analyzer

Conversations or actions that irritate or annoy thinkers/analyzers include people who present their ideas based on feelings without the facts to back them up. You know, people who speak off the cuff who have no expertise on something or people who jump into projects without planning the minute details as well as random planning or reacting without planning or worse, changing the plan and going a new direction after all the planning is finished. A few other things that annoy thinkers/analyzers are jumping around in conversation, "squirrel" kinds of distraction drives them crazy, and not being given ample time to respond to questions. Now the average person gives about ½ a second to one second response time after asking a question, which is that moment I gave you right there, about ½ a second, whereas the average person needs about two seconds. For example, if I asked you to think about this statement, pause, pause, pause, pause, pause, pause…that right there I just gave you is about two seconds. The thinker/analyzer needs about three to four seconds response time, pause, pause, pause, pause, pause, pause, pause, pause, pause, pause, pause, and pause. And that's what three to four seconds sounds like. It can seem like an eternity. On a quick side-note, a direct person only needs about ½ a second, so with that in mind, let's move on.

Challenge 7: How to Communicate with the Thinker/Analyzer

The final tip with the thinker/analyzer is the best way to communicate with them. Be logical, linear, and sequential and give your opinions only if they are based on facts, not your feelings. As for tone, tempo, and body language, lean towards a more mono-tone, or neutral tone, speak at a slower rate, similar to how I was just speaking for this section, and be more relaxed in your stance and body language without a lot of movement unless you are demonstrating something relevant to your point. We've covered direct people and thinkers/analyzers; now let's move to social extroverts.

The Social Extrovert

Challenge 1: Personality of the Social Extrovert

As I already mentioned, social extroverts are more emotional or feeling-based. They draw a lot of their motivation, or lack thereof, from their feelings. They are natural motivators or cheerleaders; they are unafraid to speak up even if they are not experts on the topic. They often draw their conclusions and voice their opinions based on their feelings, hunches, or what they believe to be logical deductions. They are quick to decide and quick to change their minds. Social extroverts tend to be impulsive, basing their decisions mostly on feelings and emotions rather than on data or research. In fact, they hate doing research or running processes, preferring to fly by the seat of their trousers.

Challenge 2: Understanding Self-Esteem/Expressions of the Social Extrovert

Some expressions of social extroverts include, "let's have fun, lets' party, go with the flow, all work no play makes one a dull person, don't worry be happy, a clean desk is a sign of a weak mind, he who dies with the most toys wins," and "don't take life too seriously!" Okay, you get the jest. Social extroverts are also very competitive, and they love to win though they'd rather have fun in the process so if they have to choose between somebody who is more competitive than them or having fun, they are going to opt to have more fun. They are natural encouragers and will sometimes embellish the truth if it makes someone feel better. They can be over complimentary and over positive, which can lead to avoidance in dealing with conflict or confrontation. Because of their high energy and creative thinking, they are great motivators and great at starting new projects or brainstorming new ideas. Social extroverts draw a lot of their self-esteem from having fun and receiving positive strokes. They thrive on compliments and positive reinforcement and are drawn to people who give them approval.

Challenge 3: Cautions of Communicating with the Social Extrovert

Some cautions of social extroverts include: they love the defining and brainstorming parts of projects but tend to get bored easy and lose interest, which leads to many unfinished projects. They want approval from their peers, but they think they don't, which leads to trying to over please certain personality styles such as direct people. This just tends to annoy direct people and gives away the power of the social extrovert. They loathe words such as "planning" or "discipline" and will do everything to avoid taking on tasks that are process or time-driven. And they think they work well under pressure with deadlines. They are quick to accept a challenge, but because they don't think through the process of time, cost, planning, and priority, they are quick to become overwhelmed and leave many tasks unfinished, which can leave team members, colleagues, and friends frustrated and confused, causing those people to quickly dismiss the abilities of social extroverts because they break their word so often and are quick to rationalize, justify, and excuse their behavior rather than recognize that they need to be more responsible and accountable.

Challenge 4: Vocations for the Social Extrovert

Some vocations that social extroverts are drawn to include: sales, marketing, public speaking, politics, theater, and music if they can be the front person such as the lead performer or anywhere they have an audience, as they thrive on attention. Social extroverts are oftentimes entrepreneurs as they love risk and adventure and hate being bound by the structure of corporate rules.

Challenge 5: Areas to Improve for the Social Extrovert

Some areas for social extroverts to improve include listening skills, yes, listening to what's in it for the other person, time management, planning and keeping your word; these are the big four areas. Also, slow down when it comes to giving your word and agreeing to things on impulse; rather, give yourself the night to think about it and/or talk with a trusted direct person, analyzer or relator to see if you might be missing something or jumping in too quickly without thinking of the impact in your life and the lives of others. You can also put little notes around your home or your office, either on your PDA, on a sticky note, or on your computer to remind you to do things such as finish what you've started, or when you find yourself getting stuck or disorganized, stop and play the "where does it go" game. This makes cleaning up fun and achievable for social extroverts rather than boring and laborious. Give yourself little rewards when you do complete something.

A bonus tip here: also give yourself a few routines to establish some grounding in your life, little things like how you start your day. Have three accomplishments scheduled before you leave the house, such as get up, get focused, and get going. Ha ha, okay, include some routines, such as making the bed, hanging up clothes, cleaning as you go. A clutter-free home leads to a clutter-free car, a clutter-free office, and a clutter-free life and frees your mind of clutter, which allows you to feel better about yourself and gives you a whole lot more creative energy to do the things you love.

Challenge 6: Irritants and Annoyances to the Social Extrovert

Conversations or actions that irritate or annoy social extroverts include ones with too many minute details or conversations that are flat and predictable and especially conversations where they don't have the opportunity to talk or give feedback. Social extroverts also get bored sitting or listening for long periods of time, which by the way, is more than 20 minutes to them, so make sure to include activities and opportunities for them to participate and be engaged in. And words such as "being disciplined" or "doing homework" need to be changed to "being consistently persistent and taking action." The results are the same; just change the words to fun and exciting ones so the social extrovert will buy into the idea.

Challenge 7: How to Communicate with the Social Extrovert

The best way to communicate with social extroverts: be animated, have fun, ask questions, and let them be involved in the process. Think of their brain as an unformatted hard drive that is waiting for the program to be written. Be consistent and be intense in a fun way to reinforce your point. Let them know how much you appreciate them, but be careful here. Only say it if you mean it; don't say it hoping it will happen. When they disappoint you, let them know – again with some intensity because if they don't feel how their actions have impacted you, they won't change. As for tone, tempo, and body language, lean towards a more assertive, almost aggressive tone. Speak at a fast rate and be confident in your stance and body language with intentional and purposeful moves and don't be afraid to interrupt them, correct them, or take back the floor from them if they are dominating a conversation; in fact, they've probably had that happen to them all their lives. And remember, have fun.

The Relational Person

Challenge 1: Personality of the Relational Person

All right, the last personality we will cover is people who are relational. Relational people are … relational. They draw a lot of their identity from relationships in and around them. They are loyal, caring, and great listeners. They are peacemakers and slow to make decisions, doing so only after careful consideration of how new decisions will impact the people around them. Because they base their decisions mostly on emotion, they will sometimes break the rules or make exceptions to accommodate people or circumstances.

Challenge 2: Understanding Self-Esteem/Expressions of the Relational Person

Some expressions of relational people include: "people are more important than projects" or "well, I suppose no one else will do it, so I'll do it" or they think to themselves, "if that person really cared about me, they'd ask me how I felt, or they'd ask me my opinion or they'd just ask me!" When in a confronting situation, they think to themselves, "I'll be the bigger person and give in." As a result, relational people often feel taken advantage of or unimportant, which can cause them to express themselves sometimes with tears or with silence when they feel threatened or backed into a corner.

They are natural encouragers, believing that even the worst person can be redeemed, and they are willing to sacrifice themselves for the cause or the big picture rather than to be selfish. Because of their caring nature and great listening abilities, people feel safe to be honest with relational people. Relational people draw a lot of their self-esteem from the things they do and the relationships they have. When they create something, it's not just their work; it's a peace of their heart. Their identity is often woven into their projects; therefore, they can feel deeply hurt if someone criticizes their work or second-guesses their motives.

Challenge 3: Cautions of Communicating with the Relational Person

Cautions of relational people include: they tend to be too flexible and can be perceived as too soft or unable to make tough decisions because they are afraid of offending anyone. This can hinder their decision making, resulting in procrastination as they can be overly cautious or constantly second-guessing themselves and their decisions, especially when involved in team projects, professionally or personally.

Challenge 4: Vocations for the Relational Person

Vocations that relational people are drawn to include human resources or human services, child care providing, taking care of pets or animals in a veterinary hospital, and the health care industry but only if they are actually working with patients side by side. You won't find very many relational surgeons, for example, but you will find a lot of relational people who are nurses or nurse assistants. Relational people also love to express themselves in writing, painting, or other quiet and creative endeavors.

Challenge 5: Areas to Improve for the Relational Person

Areas to improve: being direct and truthful rather than avoiding and being polite. For example, if you are a relational person, the next time someone answers their mobile phone in the middle of a conversation with you, instead of saying, "that's okay" when they hang up the phone, let them know you'd like their undivided attention and ask them if you can both agree on silencing your phones for the rest of the meeting. Now, I know this will feel challenging if you are a relational person the first time you try this, but if you don't, people will continue to disrespect you and your time. Though relational people are great listeners, they need to know when to cut people off.

Again, be truthful here and listen perhaps up to two to three minutes if you have that time, and then let that person know in order to give them the attention their issue deserves; then you will need to set up an appointment to finish this up. Again, I know this will be hard for you if you are a relational person. The reality is if you don't, then people won't respect you or your time and you will constantly find that you are feeling yourself being taken advantage of.

Challenge 6: Irritants and Annoyances to the Relational Person

Conversations or actions that irritate or annoy relational people include: being told, "It's nothing personal; it's just business." They hate that! Or being told, "Don't make a big deal of things," or "don't take things personally," or "don't be too sensitive." Though they won't say it, they also hate it when people are multi-tasking during a conversation with them. They would rather have the person stop and give their undivided attention even if it's only for three minutes rather than multi-task. That full attention makes all the difference to a relational person. And as for changing plans, even though relational people will tell you it's okay to cancel on them at the last minute, the truth is this deeply offends them and causes them to feel unappreciated and undervalued, which in turn will cause them to lose trust and respect for you.

Challenge 7: How to Communicate with the Relational Person

The best way to communicate with relational people: be nice, really . . . . just be nice and sincere and keep your word. Listen and take the time to give one-on-one attention, even if it is for a few short minutes. When asking relational people questions, ask, "How do you feel about this?" rather than "What do you think about this?" As for tone, tempo, and body language, lean towards a more passive tone or a softer tone, speak at a slower rate, and be very at ease in your stance and your body language, standing or sitting in a relaxed manner or a 45-degree angle. Use soft or gentle gestures, nothing grandiose or over the top, real similar to the style I've been speaking for this past short section.

Conclusion

So, now you have a better understanding of the four personality styles and how they impact your communication. You have also probably recognized some strengths as well as cautions to your dominant personality style, whether you are a direct person, a thinker/analyzer, a social extrovert, or a relational person. Though everyone is a blend of all four styles, most people have one or two dominant styles that they express, especially under pressure. At this point, the average communicator is satisfied in knowing their personality style and enough about the other styles to become a better communicator, but if you don't want to be just average, then let's take it to the next level. You see, if you learn to recognize and communicate successfully in all four styles while being flexible in your style, then you will be able to do as Dale Carnegie said, "win friends and influence people."

Look at some of the great communicators of our time who have spent a lifetime mastering the different communication styles: Zig Ziglar, Brian Tracy, Joel Osteen, Oprah Winfrey, and even Mother Teresa who said, by the way, and I quote, "people are unreasonable, illogical, and self-centered; love them anyway." When we love someone in our communication, it means we are being patient and kind, not boastful or proud. It means we are not putting others down or seeking our own selfish motives. It means we are not easily angered and we are not bringing up the other person's record of wrongs.

When we love someone in our communication, it means our words bring protection, and our words develop trust. They encourage hope and they always persevere, seeking not to bring harm or destruction into someone's life, but rather to bring truth and life. We can do this by listening and speaking their language. We learn about them, their desires, their goals, and their dreams as we speak to them in their style, no matter how different, difficult, unreasonable, or illogical they may seem.

You see, when you take the time to communicate with people in their personality style, you are also in a sense speaking their language. Think about it; if you have ever traveled abroad, especially to a country where they speak a foreign language, the more you learn of that language the better able you are to communicate your needs and desires and the more fulfilling and purposeful your trip will be. Compare that to traveling somewhere and just showing up without a map or a translation book or even without an understanding of the culture. That type of traveler spends most of their journey feeling frustrated, confused, and lost. So, whether it's communication or travel, ultimately the right style is learning to communicate fluently in all four personality styles, whether you are a direct person, a thinker/analyzer, a social extrovert, or even a relational person.

We have explored the seven challenges and how to recognize and overcome those challenges with yourself and with the people you are communicating with so that you can communicate with success.

I want to thank you for letting me spend this time with you, and until next time, I am Dawn Jones, encouraging you to live your God-given dreams.

———————————•◦•—————————

As the applause died down, Jack looked down at his paper of Key Points that he jotted down as Dawn was speaking:

Key Points from Dawn Jones' Presentation

- How do I respond in pressure situations? Am I personally Pro-Active or Reactive?
- Everyone is a blend of all four styles but usually use one or two dominant styles when in pressure situations. Which style do I align the best with when under pressure?
- Communicate to people the way they need it, not the way I would prefer to communicate with them. Adapt to their personality.

Chapter Nine

The Psychology of Conversion: What Makes Consumers Buy Online

By Bryan Heathman

As Jack pulled out of his driveway, he instinctively turned on the radio. He quickly twisted the tuning nob on the radio of his burgundy twelve-year-old Toyota Camry. There, he found it. The 55 KRC morning show host began to talk. "Well, good morning Cincinnati. Do we have a treat for you today. With us is Bryan Heathman. Bryan is the President of Made For Success out in the Seattle area. He is going to talk with us today on the psychology of why people buy goods and services online. So, if you are a salesperson or run a business, then this segment is for you. Welcome Bryan...."

————————•••••————————

The average consumer is exposed to 3,000 advertising messages - A DAY. With this much information overload, how can you succeed in getting your message across to your audience?

In 1995, the amount of content (books, articles, radio, TV, blogs, etc.) produced in a 24-hour period would take the average person a LIFETIME to review. Today, enough content is produced EACH SECOND for a lifetime of consumption by the average human being.

With the amount of content choices so overwhelming, it is important to understand the psychology of information processing in order to build a Conversion Marketing strategy that works effectively. The same principles offered in this chapter about online marketing apply to face-to-face selling. Pay close attention to the 16 practical psychological Conversion Tips presented in this chapter to help increase your close ratios either online, face-to-face, or in selling to a committee.

So, let's start looking at how the human brain processes information and deals with an overload of stimuli. The mind will create filters when processing information. These filters act as barriers to all the messages competing for mindshare. These barriers are the things that keep us sane. Understanding how to work WITH these psychological barriers is key to selling success.

We all put up barriers to messaging, called Communication Barriers. We look for messages that confirm our outlook, our worldview, our philosophy on life, our interests, etc. We filter out messages that we deem irrelevant to our viewpoints. Let's explore how to view Conversion in terms of breaking through these Communication Barriers, such as crafting messages that are consistent with the worldview of your target audience.

Importance of Identifying Your Target Audience

Understanding exactly WHO your target audience is constitutes the first step in the Psychology of Conversion. Once you have your target audience in-mind, you can then cater your campaign to an individual (or set of individuals in your mind's eye). We start by establishing the Demographic profile of an audience by formulating a clear picture of who our audience is:

- Age
- Education profile
- Gender
- Geographic location
- Marital status
- Household income
- Residence (renter, home owner, condo dweller, etc.)

Every now and then, I have made classic marketing mistakes. Let me tell you about a miscalculation in order to help you prevent making similar missteps related to demographic profiling.

A while back, I created an eCommerce website using a dark graphic treatment (i.e. black). After operating this site for a year, we discovered that the typical consumer of this service was 75% female. According to design specialists who deal in color theory, using dark graphics are a detriment to attracting and motivating this demographic.

By changing the user interface to softer colors and more descriptive copywriting, we were able to generate a 50% increase in our Visitor to Buyer ratios. The questions I ask myself include: How much revenue did I sacrifice as a result of this design misstep? How many advertising dollars did I waste driving the wrong target audience to this website?

Convert Website Visitors to Buyers

Next, once you can visualize your target audience(s), it is essential to understand their outlook on life, their view of themselves, their recreational pursuits, and other factors that make them tick. Marketers call this the Psychographic Profile of your target audience.

To understand what a Psychographic profile looks like, here are questions to ask to help understand your customer's personality, values, attitudes, interests, or lifestyles:

- What do they do in their spare time? For example, there are powerful correlations between software professionals and road bikes, between mathematicians and music, between mechanics and viewing motor sports and between corporate executives and golf.
- What are their beliefs?
- What is their social status?
- What lifestyle do they lead?
- What strong opinions do they hold?
- What are their values?

Once you have completed your demographic and psychographic profiles on the ideal target audience(s), the next principle to add to the knowledge base on Conversion Marketing is the concept of SOCIAL INFLUENCE.

Social Influence is a deep-seated human desire to appear consistent with what we have already done in the past, as well as commitments that define the things we represent in the future. This human desire is so deep-rooted, that we will even do things that are contrary to our financial best interests in order to act consistently with what we feel we represent.

The principle of Social Influence means we will convince ourselves of the correctness of a decision, even if the decision is not in-line with our best interests. So, to stay true to our nature, to be consistent with our inner convictions, the human mind goes into a "mental auto-pilot mode" in order to speed up our internal decision-making process, all in the blink of an eye. This fundamental aspect of human nature helps us process the bombardment of messages by disregarding messages inconsistent with our inner convictions, worldview/philosophy.

How can you structure your Conversion Marketing messaging to conform to the "mental auto-pilot" mode of your target audience?

FIRST: clearly understand your target audience – both their demographic and psychographic profile.

SECOND: create messaging and imagery that is consistent with the outlook of your target audience. For instance, if you are targeting Empty Nesters (50-63 years old) you would use inspirational messages and images consistent with their outlook: happy grandchildren, RV travel to National Parks, beach vacations, spas, or wine tasting.

THIRD: pick your "call to action" eCommerce strategy from a list of options that support the desire to be consistent with your target audiences' nature. Pick the appropriate promotional tool, which can be found in the book *Conversion Marketing* by Bryan Heathman. Then, carefully review the Conversion Tips listed in this chapter for techniques that influence buying behavior.

Psychological Conversion Tips

This series of Conversion Tips originates from carefully researched psychological studies on human behavior, which have proven to generate hundreds of millions of dollars in eCommerce conversions by skilled Conversion Marketers. Think carefully about each Tip and how it can be adapted into your eCommerce environment. Don't be surprised to see a spike in conversion rates when you implement these powerful psychological triggers in the design of your campaigns.

Conversation Tip 1: Start Small

If your ultimate goal is to sell something large and relatively expensive, it is rare that your company will achieve success in an eCommerce environment on the first, second, or even third visit to your website. Therefore, you need to build a bond of trust with your audience by performing a small transaction, and then build your way into a large commitment. For instance, if you are selling a $25,000 Mediterranean cruise package, think about offering a short weekend trip as a trial to build trust and whet the appetite of your audience.

Conversation Tip 2: Stepped Commitments

Create a gradual series of commitments, tapping into the latent "power of consistency" behavior in the human mind. Set the stage for creating a series of automatic conversion behavior on your website. Start with small commitments such as opting-in for a newsletter, direct-mail campaign, or other informational series of messages. These small commitments will impact the self-image of your audience, and will help them see their viewpoint as consistent with that of your company.

Conversation Tip 3: The Magic of Written Declarations

Recently, I developed a website in the industry of Audio Publishing. One consistent message coming from this industry's leading celebrity speakers like Brian Tracy, Chris Widener, and Zig Ziglar, is in setting clear and definable goals. There is great power in written goals, proven in study after study. One study found that two percent of Harvard graduates have written goals. These two percent of graduates consistently out-earn their non-goal-setting counterparts by significant margins. Why? It gets back to the human need to be consistent with one's beliefs. The act of writing a goal deeply seats this commitment in the mind. So, how do you get people to make written declarations online? Here are a few ideas:

- Testimonial Sweepstakes: offer your target audience a chance to win a big prize by submitting a testimonial to your product/service, such as a "Why I like _____" statement. This helps your audience go on record endorsing your product or service.
- Easter Egg Campaign – an "Easter egg" is a hidden message within a website or product. Run a contest where you prompt people to find your "Easter egg" message (i.e. as hidden on the back of the product label, nested in an email newsletter, nested within your home page, or in icons placed throughout your website). Have the contest be contingent on finding the message and submitting it online. Craft your message so that it states a positive testimonial for your product. When submitted, it enters them in the contest and also embeds the positive message in the contestant's mind.

Examples: Craft your hidden messages as a written declaration supporting your product.

- I love this product!
- Your product rocks!

Psychological studies have shown that people who make written declarations will more assertively defend these positions than research subjects who only made mental commitments. These strong convictions hold for the subjects who made written declarations even when they were shown evidence to challenge their position.

Conversation Tip 4: Social Proof

Publish testimonials from people who fit the demographic or psychographic profile of your target audience. The idea is to show support for your products/services by people who look "just like me." Use integrity with this tip, and ask your best customers for real testimonials. You will be surprised what people have to say, and you just may learn a thing or two about your product/service.

The more you can demonstrate that many people support your idea/product/service as correct, the more others will perceive your idea/product/service as correct. Think of the highest profile success story of this technique the next time you see a McDonald's sign showing how many billions of customers have been served.

Conversation Tip 5: Extra Effort to Join a Club

The more effort that a person applies into a commitment, the greater is your ability to influence the attitude and beliefs of club members.

How can you apply this principle to an eCommerce environment?

Offer a free newsletter, but require the extra effort of a double opt-in to join the newsletter.

When launching a new website, communicate a compelling promise or purpose that a membership will achieve but require a waiting period for "approval" before validating the membership. This impression of exclusivity increases the perceived value of your site. Think of the example of a waiting period before joining a country club, or a review from a membership committee before new applications are accepted.

Require a referral from an already existing member before you allow new members to "join the club." This was successful for Google's launch of its Gmail service to compete with Microsoft's Hotmail version of a free email account. Not only was a Gmail account sought-after, but it was also a badge of prestige for early users because they were on the inside elite of the high-tech community.

Conversation Tip 6: Loss Leader

Offering a loss leader is a tried-and-true method of attracting new business in the hyper-competitive, brick & mortar retail world. Grocery stores operate loss leaders all the time – for example, in North America discounted turkeys around Thanksgiving, discounted soft drinks prior to July 4th, and candy discounts prior to Halloween.

What are the biggest shopping holidays in your country or region? These deeply discounted items attract shoppers for the Loss Leader, which is made up in the volume of other items purchased during the same season. Think about your product profile and offering seasonal discounts on highly popular items as a way of attracting new customers.

Conversation Tip 7: Ask an Expert

The influence of a well-known expert in your field can project a positive influence on your company. Offer a Blog, where your website visitors can interact with an Expert/Celebrity/Leader in your field. The value of the interaction and ability to read unscripted feedback, plus the residual benefit of repeat traffic to your website, can have a very positive impact on your visitors.

Conversation Tip 8: Referrals

Research has proven that people prefer to say "Yes" to a purchase when coming from someone they know and/or like.

Provide an incentive item for people who refer a required number of friends to your website to join your newsletter or purchase items. Here are a few working examples from past campaigns offered by various Internet marketers.

1. Get 10 additional sweepstakes entries for each friend you refer who enters a sweepstakes for a free trip to New Orleans. This was deployed by the State tourism commission in Louisiana for years to build a database of hundreds of thousands of people interested in traveling to Louisiana.
2. Earn a free movie rental certificate for every five new newsletter opt-ins. One marketer was able to save 50% on new customer acquisition costs by leveraging this technique.
3. Get a free sample package of Proctor & Gamble personal care products for each friend referred to a sweepstakes. This referral structure served double duty to accomplish the objective of gaining new traffic and newsletter opt-ins, and achieving the objectives of the product trial.

Conversation Tip 9: Attractiveness Factor

People naturally tend to respond positively to people and graphic design elements that match their tastes. If you use a celebrity spokesperson to promote your items, then select one that inspires your target audience.

If you market items where it is cost prohibitive to leverage a celebrity spokesperson, then spend some of your energy on the graphic design of your website that closely aligns with the "attractiveness factor" of your target audience. Think carefully about the color scheme you choose and the design elements and style of copywriting used to stimulate the senses of your target audience.

Celebrity Endorsements: One example of using the "Attractiveness Factor" to stimulate their target audience was a major search engine that was focused on attracting young males from 18-29 years old. They ran a sweepstakes where each entry earned a chance to meet a very attractive 19-year-old tennis sensation.

The winner of this sweepstakes was a 21-year-old college student, who brought four friends to meet the tennis star while on the beach during a swimsuit modeling photo session. We were all greatly amused when the winner of the sweepstakes presented the tennis star with a bouquet of roses to win her eye! If you are curious how the tennis star responded, she politely declined the offer with a wink and a smile.

Models: To create a positive association with your products, it can be effective and economical for smaller companies to pose an attractive model next to product images in your online catalog.

Conversation Tip 10: Social Responsibility: Leveraging the 'Us-Versus-Them' Phenomenon

People have the tendency to mentally group themselves into associations with clubs, charities, movements, and organizations. The obvious illustration of this phenomenon is rooting for the home team in football or baseball. Residents of cities where teams reside adopt an Us-Versus-Them mentality on game day and will feverishly cheer for their home team.

This phenomenon can be activated by giving to charitable organizations that share an affinity with your target audience. The association your company has can align you with common goals of your target audience. Some people choose to buy certain products because of their associations with organizations in which they strongly believe in.

One company that promotes language-learning software offers five percent of the proceeds from each purchase to support "green" initiatives for environmental causes. This company has proven this tool to be effective selling "National Geographic" software products, where satisfied consumers have indicated their purchase decision based solely on the company's social stance to charitable giving! So pick a charity that you feel good about that also aligns with your target audience and start giving back.

A local karate studio organizes a quarterly "Pizza and Game Night" at the studio where parents drop off kids and enjoy a night out on the town. One hundred percent of the money collected goes to building elaborate play sets for orphaned children in disadvantaged areas. One reason they succeed is by helping their customers participate in socially responsible activities. With programs that appeal to a cause bigger than oneself, it is no coincidence that this karate studio is one of the top five largest single-location karate studios in North America.

Conversation Tip 11: The Draw of 'Authority'

Authority figures can have a strong influence on your target audience. Interesting studies have been run where people have been encouraged to perform activities contrary to their beliefs and values based solely on the influence of an "authority figure" telling them that the actions are justified.

Notice the types of Hollywood celebrities who are hired to endorse products. Just recently, I saw an actor who plays a respectable President of the United States in a popular television series. In this television spot, the actor is promoting "You are in good hands..." for a large insurance company. Actors who play physicians are often used to promote products/services of large advertisers as the positive impression people have towards physicians, in general, will extend to the advertiser's message.

In an eCommerce environment, leveraging authority figures can have a measurable effect on your conversion rates with website visitors. People will inherently trust the message coming from these celebrity figures.

In the absence of the big-budget dollars to hire a celebrity, send an email to a leading authority in your industry who presented at a recent trade event or authored a book relevant to your industry. Many experts, including professional speakers and authors, are MORE than happy to associate their message to your audience, as the goal of public relations is always top of mind for speakers and authors.

Conversation Tip 12: Graphic Design

In the physical world, people respond to non-verbal cues, such as the title before someone's name, clothes, uniforms, or visible status symbols (cars, homes, watches, jewelry, designer logos), that communicate authority. In the eCommerce environment, you can communicate the trust associated with such visible cues via the graphic design of your website. Carefully pick color schemes and design elements that support your product.

Conversation Tip 13: Scarcity Creates Demand

While studying for my undergraduate degree in Economics, the principle of "Scarcity creates Demand" was taught as yet another dry lesson from the thick Economics textbook. When it is perceived that a product is in high demand and there is limited supply, people tend to stock-up or purchase in advance of their need.

Here are a few tips for creating Demand by communicating a scarce availability of product and/or price (which Economists called "Artificial Scarcity"):

- Limited time discount – act now while the discount applies
- Limited quantity – buy a limited supply of discounted products, i.e. available to the first 50 customers
- Commemoratives – Artists, by creating numbered series of collectable works, are the masters of this conversion technique. Authors also leverage this phenomenon by offering a limited quantity of signed books or by organizing "signing events" at local bookstores and trade events.

Conversation Tip 14: Scarcity Plus Rivalry

The concept of creating scarcity with the added element of a rivalry for the scarce goods is the essence of the eBay auction-based business model. A limited quantity of items plus a huge network of deal-hunters are the perfect convergence of the Scarcity + Rivalry principle to stimulate demand for conversions.

eBay auctions offer valued items in limited discounts for a limited time, typically offered at a VERY low initial asking price. As rivals for these discounted products start to compete, a frenzy of activity is initiated that would not normally exist for the same item at full price or even at a reasonable discount. As rivals become emotionally involved in the purchase process, they will bid up the price of items often to the full price (or beyond) in their quest to "win" the auction. The Emotional Involvement associated with the rivalry can have a powerful impact on your conversion rates.

While I was in college, I posted a classified ad for a popular-sized carpet used in the building where I lived. As it happens, two motivated buyers showed up to buy the carpet at the exact same time, giving me a front-row seat on consumer behavior related to Scarcity + Rivalry. I watched these two potential buyers bid up the carpet fifty percent over the asking price in order to take advantage of this scarce item. How can this principle apply to your business?

Think about creating a store on eBay or Craigslist to promote a limited supply of your goods and services at a discount. The Emotional Involvement associated with the rivalry can have a powerful impact on your conversion rates. Stores are relatively intuitive to set up and populate your catalog. You will gain the substantial advantage of gaining access to the massive amount of traffic going to these ecommerce websites daily. If the process of setting up your own stores on these websites is too time consuming or daunting, there are a number of people who are experienced eBay practitioners who offer the service of selling your products through these online retailers for a percentage of revenue, a percentage of gross margin, or by buying your goods at wholesale discounts. eBay also has a network of Trading Assistants who will train you on the subtle tips and tricks of selling on eBay. These Trading Assistants can be found in many major cities for a fairly reasonable hourly fee.

Conversation Tip 15: Product Collections

If you offer a catalog of products with a wide array of choices, you can simplify the decision-making process for your customers by offering pre-packaged products, often sold at a discount. It is proven that a certain percentage of the population will buy a larger dollar amount of product if it will save them time and money sorting through all the options of products on your website.

One successful online retailer will do 10% of their business overall offering a $999 package deal on all their products (which individually sell for $10-$25 separately). A discount offered on the package deal can be structured to leverage this technique properly.

Conversation Tip 16: Cognitive Dissonance

'Cognitive Dissonance' is a marketing term that describes conflicting thoughts that some consumers experience after making a big purchase. When confronted with a big purchase decision, some consumers will feel a sense of regret called "post-purchase dissonance" for making the purchase, spending the money, or discovering information that makes them uncomfortable with their purchase.

Techniques can be used to help minimize this effect, and help increase conversion rates on your website prior to purchase. Here are tips on how to structure an eCommerce site to minimize this "objection":

- Create a "No-hassle" return policy
- Offer a 100% money-back guarantee
- Provide easy access to Customer Service, via email or a toll-free number
- Offering a credit card payment option helps alleviate this concern as consumers know they can dispute charges and receive a credit on their account from their credit card issuers.

In our increasingly fast-paced, information-laden society, your target audience's ability to make a buying decision for your product/service requires creating prompts that trigger a normal and predictable feeling within the mind of your audience.

The more reliable the cues you can provide in your eCommerce environment will help break down the natural barriers we use to protect our minds from the bombardment of information presented each day.

As I speak to you by phone today, I'm sipping an espresso in a coffee shop in a small resort town deep in the heart of the Washington State wine country. In being intentional about letting a few marketing messages penetrate my conscious mind, I can count at least 10 marketing messages competing for my attention at a casual glance (Coca-Cola, Good Humor ice cream, flip flops, sunglasses, resort wear, etc.). Your job is to create a mentally comfortable experience for your website visitors in order to capture attention, gain permission, and start the repetition of your Branding message.

For more practical tips on converting visitors into buyers, look for the book, ebook, or audiobook of *Conversion Marketing* by Bryan Heathman everywhere books are sold.

As the radio show went to commercial, Jack pondered, "What if…what if I became an expert marketer too? Sales and marketing do go hand in hand. I am on to something here. I am going to have to look up this Bryan Heathman and see if I can have a conversation with him."

Chapter Ten

How to Own the Closing Zone

By Dr. Allan Colman

A round noon on Wednesday, Jack pulled into the Wal-Mart Super Center on Cincinnati-Dayton Road in West Chester, OH. It was a nice day. Very sunny and 82 degrees.

In the Wal-Mart was one of Jack's favorite fast food restaurants. A Subway sandwich shop. He walked in and ordered his lunch and then sat down at a table. As he unfolded his lunch, he reached into his backpack and pulled out a new book he had just purchased the other day. It was a compilation of multiple sales experts. It was titled *Sales Success.* He opened the book to Chapter Ten, which was written by Dr. Allan Colman. The chapter was titled *How to Own the Closing Zone.* Jack began to read.

———————————•●●●•———————————

Anyone who desires to be a sales leader or efficient marketer must refine his or her closing skills. Many people are experienced with getting their feet in the door. Some people are even quite successful in developing new leads on a regular basis. But completing the cycle by turning proposals and pitches into signed contracts takes a corporate approach that only a few have mastered but all can learn and implement. This chapter discusses successful closing strategies and ideas so that you can own the closing zone.

We often tell our consulting clients, "Stop planning. Start closing." The reason for this is simple: Marketing strategies are an essential step in creating awareness about your firm or your practice, but you must also take action, engage with your prospects, and close more business.

That doesn't mean that some planning isn't required. One often overlooked area of new business development is taking the time to identify your prospects' needs so that when you meet them one on one – when you're in what we call the Closing Zone – you're ready.

Here are a few key questions to answer before going into the meeting:

- What internal pressures is your client or prospect facing?
- What services and activities does your prospect consider vital and essential?
- Who are their competitors and what new products or services are out there?

When we work with our clients to help them prepare to close more sales, we take the time to explore and fully answer these and related questions. Having a list of prospects is great; validating each prospect's potential and having a customized game plan for each meeting is even better.

Beginning to End

While many people assume that closing is what happens at the end of the sales process, the reality is that closing starts with the very first contact or meeting and then continues with every subsequent communication.

Understanding that closing is a process and not a milestone means that, in order to facilitate the process, you must always be working to set up the next contact and keep the relationship growing. There are a few important skills you'll want to master along the closing path:

- **Have multiple points of contact within the client's group**: Don't limit yourself to one way in; develop many relationships simultaneously.
- **Get to know the client's executives whenever possible:** Remember that the client's C-suite can have a big impact on retention choices.
- **Be efficient, not greedy**: Focus on providing value in every stage of the closing process rather than pushing too hard toward the sale.
- **Be confident**: Enter the closing process with a positive mindset that will shine through to your prospective client.

123

- **Define client focus and what it means to be "client-centric"**: Speak in benefits, not features, and anticipate and address client concerns with their best interests in mind.
- **Keep clients informed**: Effective communication is key to the closing process. Don't leave clients guessing.
- **Differentiate yourself from competitors by talking strategy and successes**: Take the opportunity to share how you have achieved results and focus on the strategic steps you took to get there.

Don't forget the importance of understanding the client's decision-making process: knowing who else might be involved, what the decision-making timing is, and what additional information might be needed. Learning the answers to these questions is a good way to keep the dialogue open, build client relationships, and move your prospects closer to closing.

Hiring the Right Business Development Consultant

In 2011, quarterback Aaron Rodgers helped the Green Bay Packers take the Vince Lombardi trophy back to Wisconsin for the first time in 14 years. But Rodgers didn't do it alone—he had the support of an entire team of players and a gentleman named Mike McCarthy, the Green Bay Packers' coach. Could Rodgers have claimed the victory without McCarthy? Maybe. But having McCarthy there to help identify weak areas, develop game-winning strategies, and offer encouragement certainly increased the Packers' chance of bringing the trophy home.

The same thing holds true for companies interested in improving business development: when you want to increase your chance of bringing home the trophy—or closing the sale—consider a business coach. A business coach can help you identify the highest-performing business development strategies, map a course for closing more sales, and reassure management that business development efforts are on the right path.

When looking for a business development consultant, here are a few things you'll want to find out:

- Do they have a track record of generating results?
- Do they have a proven process for identifying sales opportunities?

- Do they offer strategies for nurturing existing clients and client retention?
- Do they give you a reasonable time frame (e.g. 90-120 days) in which you will be able to see results?
- Do they emphasize closing skills?"

If your business development consultant can answer "yes" to the above questions—like we can here at the Closers Group—you're on your way toward the Closing Zone and bringing home the trophy—the closed sale. If they hesitate, or can't answer one of the questions above, you may want to consider finding a replacement to help lead your team to victory. Feel free to contact us if we can help.

Divide and Conquer: Distinguishing Yourself and Closing the Deal

No two clients are the same. When getting to know your prospects – or looking for additional business from existing clients – it's important to accept this reality. Tailoring questions and presentations to fit the client's needs, personality, and industry will separate you from your competitors. Before the meeting, do your research to ensure quality work and questions. This will ensure that you're at your best in the Closing Zone.

Here are a number of questions that you should consider asking at every meeting:

- How will the work be handled between you and the client's company?
- What forms of communication does the client prefer?
- How often do they prefer communication?
- Who will be the day-to-day point of contact at the company?

Your interest in day-to-day operations will show your eagerness to jump right in and start working. But how do you tailor questions specific to the client? Refer back to your research. Edit and add questions as necessary. Corporate clients will have different needs than a small, private company. Don't treat them as one in the same!

The hard part comes next: listening. Both talking and listening lead to closing the deal. Building and diversifying your closing skills will lead to more business and better client relationships.

Breaking Down the Course

Competitive alpine skiers – whether they focus on downhill, the slalom, the giant slalom, or the super-G – know that in order to achieve their goals, they need a specific action plan. In the case of alpine skiing at the Winter Olympics, that action plan starts by determining which events the skier will race and then moves on to focus on breaking down the course, identifying the right path to make the jump or turn, and analyzing the terrain and conditions in order to ensure that – when they arrive at the bottom of the hill – they produce a winning time.

When sports' analysts comment on the downhill events, their focus is on two things: what individual skiers are doing that sets themselves apart and the terrain of the course.

Business development consultants have a similar focus. Their expert commentary and guidance helps sales and marketing professionals successfully analyze the terrain of client meetings and relationships. They are also good at analyzing what makes each professional or business unique.

Every business has something that sets it apart. For some, the differentiating factor is a heightened level of client knowledge. When this is the case, all of the components of business development training dovetail.

If you're having difficulty pinning down what makes you different, a business development consultant can help you identify it and work with you to build a strategy around that difference. If you're looking to improve your closing skills and take your sales strategy to the next level, a consultant can help you identify the best strategies for evaluating the options available to you, choose the right path for your presentations, and work with you to ensure that you stay on course and sign new clients in record time.

Staying in Shape During Off-Season

While the action may not be on the diamond, don't think that there isn't activity during baseball's off-season. Owners, managers, and coaches are making behind-the-scenes changes that will help build the team's strengths, develop new offensive strategies based on their players (and those who they'll be facing once the season is underway), and preparing for the action. Players are doing their best to stay in shape as well so that, once Spring Training is underway, they'll be ready to perform when the time comes to step up to the plate.

Like the red zone football where the offense needs to stay focused and persevere toward the end zone, baseball's batters need to step into the box in order to score. Studying the opposing pitcher's patterns and form – along with good, old-fashioned practice – are crucial parts of success. Still, no matter how much power a hitter has, often strikeouts precede hits and runs. That's where perseverance comes into play.

Persistence also pays off when you're engaged in marketing. An attorney client of ours had held several meetings with an Assistant General Counsel at a university in her area. When this AGC was promoted to General Counsel, our client asked my advice about how to proceed now that her prospect was twice as busy. I suggested she offer to provide backup support, filling in at the GC's former position until a replacement could be found. Not only did her prospect take her up on the offer, but additional engagements were also lined up.

Had she not been to the plate several times to develop her closing skills, and learned her prospect's best moves, she would not have been ready to hit this one out of the park.

Excelling in the Red Zone

It was perhaps the best NFL game of the year, where the Indianapolis Colts came from behind with less than a minute to play, beating the New England Patriots by a single point. Watching the game, it was clear that neither team was willing to quit—both team's offenses and defenses played their hearts out.

The number of times each of these teams scored when entering the red zone demonstrates just how important it is to persevere and to never say it can't be done. That same 'never quit' sense of commitment should be practiced by the sales leadership at your company. Just because your proposal wasn't selected, your firm did not make it on a company's panel, or you couldn't get that client meeting you wanted, don't quit. Periodically contact the prospect in order to keep your name in front of them. That way, when it comes for his business to replace their current firm or bring in a legal specialist, you'll be considered again.

Going to the World Series

Each year, Major League Baseball's World Series is a reminder of the importance of developing strong closing skills. Regardless of which teams make it to the "big dance," the players to watch are the power hitters and the closing pitchers. This year, the Philadelphia Phillies returned to the series, but the power of the hitters and the closing skills of the New York Yankees pitchers combined to dethrone last year's champs.

Just as strong closing pitchers are critical to an MLB team's success, closing skills are crucial for business success. Whatever analogy you use when you're making an important pitch to a prospect, it's important to focus on the close. Perhaps one of the most underutilized tactics for closing involves simply having an agenda.

When you're invited to the big dance and have an opportunity to generate more business -- whether an informal dinner meeting to discuss future opportunities with a current client or a formal RFP response – take the time to talk with your prospect ahead of time. Indicate what you believe will be important and be sure to identify your prospect's ideas and priorities. Focus on each of these areas, practice your responses to possible questions, consider different approaches, anticipate what might be "thrown at you," and even ask your business development consultant to play devil's advocate and introduce additional scenarios.

The preparation that you put into a meeting will ensure that you're ready for the big event. After the handshakes and greetings, "warm up" by reviewing the agenda with your client or prospect. Ask them if anything new has become opportunity or a challenge for them, get their input on the importance of discussion items and involve them in agreeing to the order in which topics will be discussed.

Think of your agenda as a playbook for the meeting – and go back to it as necessary to adjust your play when they throw a curveball or count on receiving a soft pitch. Make sure that your bases are covered throughout the meeting – focus on addressing all of their questions and needs, and don't be afraid to swing for the fence and ask when their decision will be made.

The more that you practice your plays, the more that your performance will improve and the more success you'll have.

Maximizing Rejection

Making it to the Finals

For the L.A. Lakers, it was a long time between championships. After being called basketball's first dynasty for early back-to-back wins, the Lakers started to see long gaps between titles. During the 2008 NBA Playoffs, the team was embarrassed by the way they lost the finals to their longtime rival the Boston Celtics. After the loss, they made a team commitment to keep at it until they won – a commitment that paid off in the 2009 finals

Similar to the Lakers' challenges, making a commitment to a comeback success is related to an often-overlooked concept in legal sales – an approach I call Maximizing Rejection. Simply put, if you don't win a proposal, are passed over for new client work, or aren't even invited to the dance, do not go in the corner and let yourself disappear. Instead, make sure that you continue to be present. As you continue to gain more experience, you will realize how important your investment with the company or agency is, and why continued follow up and follow through is so worthwhile.

Things not going your way? Here are some suggestions on turning things around:

- If another company has been selected, call back to follow up with your prospect in 3-4 months.
- Remind prospective clients that you look forward to working with them in the future, and ask if they are getting what they expected and what they need from the firm that was hired.
- Keep prospects who have received proposals on your "touch" list and make sure to follow through with a contact 2-3 times a year.
- Consider inviting them to be on a panel with you at an upcoming professional event—it's a great way to reconnect.

Practicing proactive sales is a matter of recognizing that the prospect made an investment in spending time with you and your proposal. They got to know you–and if you were close in the finals, keeping in touch will enhance the prospect of future work. Don't give up – stick with your commitment to your prospects, continue doing your best work, and close the sale.

The Amazing Spider-Man

No matter how many times Spider-Man was knocked down, captured, delayed, or rejected, he found a way to get through the situation and to win the fight

Maximizing rejection is an extension of this lesson – one that this business development consultant emphasizes to clients. Just because your proposal is not the one chosen doesn't mean that you don't still have a future prospect.

Instead of giving up when you don't close the sale, try the following:

- Analyze your process to determine the reasons why your sales effort was less than successful. Learn from this experience and use the knowledge you gain the next time that you're making a pitch.
- Follow up with the prospect after 3-6 months have passed. Asking how the engagement is going will let them know you still want to work with them, and that you're interested in keeping in touch.

Regular contact helps improve your chances of being retained in the future. Don't give up: remember, Spidey eventually got his man – and you can close more business if you follow his lead, and continue to pursue your prospects.

————————•●●•————————

As Jack finished up his ham and cheese sub, he placed his bookmark back in his book and closed it. "That was a good chapter," thought Jack. "Very helpful." He pulled out his sales planner and opened it to his notes section. He began to write.

Action Steps from *How to Own the Closing Zone* with Dr. Allan Colman

- Everyone needs a coach. Even Aaron Rodgers and Michael Jordan looked to their coaches for advice. Digger Jones is a great coach for me.
- Tailor my selling questions to match the prospect's needs, personality, and industry.

- Stay in selling shape. Like an athlete in the off-season, I can't afford to let my selling muscles get flabby. I will read one sales book per month and build more muscle.
- Stay persistent like Spider Man. If I don't get the sale today, don't give up. Re-connect with the prospect a few weeks down the road. Create value for them and they will come.

Conclusion

Eight months later:

Jack opened his door at the glorious Grand Hyatt Hotel in New York City to head down to breakfast. As he stepped out, crunching directly under his feet was the blue and white logo of the USA Today newspaper the hotel staff had left for him. Jack picked it up, only wrinkled slightly, and headed for the elevator.

Jack and the rest of his Cincinnati sales team for that matter were in Manhattan for their company's national sales convention. All toll, there would be over five thousand sales representatives converging on the Grand Hyatt.

Jack walked into the brightly lit restaurant and was escorted by a young man dressed in sharp black pants, a black dress vest, and a sparkling white long sleeve shirt that didn't have a wrinkle in sight. The young man motioned his arm toward a table in the middle of a row of small two-seaters in the middle of the restaurant. It was lavishly set with a sparkling white table cloth, a water goblet, an obviously china coffee mug, and a set of gold-plated silverware. The restaurant was a little cool in temperature but not uncomfortable.

Jack liked to eat breakfast alone. It was a time where he could read, pray, and reflect on his thoughts.

After he placed his order of oatmeal, wheat toast, a banana, and apple juice, Jack turned his attention to his USA Today. "I wonder if my favorite column is in this paper?" Jack thought to himself.

Jack immediately skipped the opening section and turned to the next section. There was a green square in the upper left hand corner that said "Money." Underneath the words, it read "Section B." If it were here, it would be in this section.

Jack scanned the first page; nothing there. He turned the page and there was his favorite column, "The Business Edge" by Mark Bowser.

Bowser's title today was very intriguing. It read "The Business Linchpin." Jack began to read.

———————————•••• •———————————

The Business Linchpin: Can It Destroy You? By **Mark Bowser**

Is there a linchpin that could start a domino effect that could devastate your business? Or, is there a tipping point that could start an avalanche of success like a runaway snowball?

Interesting questions, but is there an answer? My wife and I love to watch the hit TV show Castle. Recently, they had an intriguing two-part episode that explored this concept of a linchpin. In the story, an economic linchpin was discovered that if put in motion would destroy the United States economy and start a downward domino effect that would lead the globe to World War III. It was a very entertaining escapade from our daily lives, and in the story, the bad guys almost succeeded? But, it got me thinking. Is it possible? Could one event so delude human reasoning and magnify emotions to the point of utter devastation?

I believe that there very well may be a linchpin or a tipping point for your business. Let's explore the linchpin first. What if you had all your eggs for success in one basket and you lost the basket? Do you see where I am going with this? Brian Tracy says that "Everything Counts" when it comes to selling. What if you or one of your associates kills (accidentally of course) the business with your largest client? What if that client composed of 85% of your annual business? Could you survive...or would it be your linchpin?

So, what is the solution? We must avoid the business error so many of us are guilty of, including myself. We put most of our eggs in one basket, and if we lose that business, we are headed towards economic devastation known as Chapter 11. We avoid it by spreading out our marketing. By kicking into high gear our prospecting for new and more clients.

The only way to avoid the business linchpin is to make sure that no one event or any one client so controls the lifeblood of your business existence. Spread it out. Market more. Do business with different size clients. That will kill the linchpin...and not you.

Now, let's talk about the tipping point. Is there a point where all your marketing, all your sales, all your success converge into a place where it spills over to tremendous, incredible visibility and success? I believe so. Why do some products go viral?

I don't think we can know the answer...but we know they do. In fact, this article may go viral, but why this one and not another one?

Your tipping point exists and it will find you...if you continue to practice business success. In fact, do more of it. Supercharge it. What will make you more visible? What will get you and your product or service more attention? How can you get your product or service into the hands of more people? How can you serve them more than you currently are? Seek the answers to these questions and take action on what you discover, and before you know it, your tipping point may find you.

As Jack read the last paragraph of the inspiring article, he popped the last bite of wheat toast into his mouth. He then proceeded to pay his bill, giving the finely tailored, polite young waiter a very generous twenty-two percent tip.

Jack then went back up to his room and brushed his teeth. He looked at his watch and said to himself, "I still have 25 minutes before I need to be in the ballroom." The National Sales Conference was being held in the beautiful Grand Ballroom of the Hyatt.

Jack sat down on the sofa in his room and began to read the Sports Section of the USA Today. "Let's see how the Reds did last night." Jack was an avid baseball fan with his favorite team of course being his beloved Cincinnati Reds. "Awesome. Six to two. Take that you Cardinals. Let's see, that puts us three and a half games up on St. Louis."

At promptly 8:51 AM, Jack stepped out of his room and headed for the ballroom. The meeting was to start at 9:00 AM sharp. Since there were so many people at the conference, all sales reps had been given tickets. Free of course.

As Jack stepped into the expansive, richly decorated space, he looked at his ticket and found his row and seat. The ballroom was already three quarters full and would fill up quickly in the next five minutes.

Jack found his row and began squeezing his way politely to his seat. He thought to himself, "This is a great seat." Jack's seat was dead center and five rows back from the stage.

Every seat in the row was taken except the seat right next to him. "I wonder who is sitting here," Jack thought to himself. As the words were forming in his mind, he saw a familiar figure make his way through the row. The older gentleman was dressed like royalty. To Jack, the man was royalty. Yes, it was Digger Jones. As Digger smiled at Jack, he stretched out his hand. His cuff linked, white shirt showed just slightly from under his stark black perfectly pressed worsted wool suit. "Big day for you, my friend," Digger said with a warm smile.

"What do you mean?" asked Jack. "In fact, what are you doing here? I mean, it is great to see you, but I wasn't expecting you at all."

"I wouldn't miss this for the world. I have been planning on attending this from that first day we met back on that bench in front of the guerrilla exhibit at the Cincinnati Zoo."

"You are more than a mystery to me, my friend," said Jack. At that, the meeting began. Mr. Frank Rohn stepped to the microphone. Frank Rohn was the company President/CEO. Rohn's appearance was a shock to the entire audience. No one was expecting him to be here.

"Good morning!" said Mr. Rohn. "It is an honor to be able to spend a few moments with you today. I didn't want to miss this. It is not often that we have a Michael Jordan of sales among us. As you know, I started with this company many, many years ago sitting in seats just like the ones you are sitting in this morning. Only, it was Chicago and not New York, and it was the Hilton instead of the Hyatt. "

"The year was 1983, and I was awarded the prize as the top salesperson of the year. Little did I know, that the record I set that year would stand for nearly thirty years. Well, I am thrilled to announce to you that it has been broken. There is one sitting among you today who has become the most extraordinary sales champion I have ever seen. Not too many months ago, his sales were dismal, and to tell you the truth, his job was on the bubble. I have been watching him closely for months like a father watches his child play baseball. I watched from the stands as he hit home run after home run. It wasn't all victory. There were many strikeouts along the way. But I smiled as I saw our champion get up from the dirt and get back into the batter's box. He is a true champion and an inspiration for us all of hard work, determination, enthusiasm, persistence, and integrity."

"Without further ado, let me introduce to you this year's sales champion and the new record holder, Jack Blake."

The crowd erupted into a standing ovation. Digger was the first on his feet. Jack was stunned. He knew he was in the top five, but he had no idea that he was number one and had broken Mr. Rohn's record.

With prodding from Digger, Jack slowly rose to his feet and made his way up to the stage. As he went, people were patting him on the back, shaking his hand, and giving him high fives.

As he reached the lectern, Mr. Rohn was smiling and clapping. He reached out his hand and shook Jack's hand as he pulled him into a bear hug. "Congratulations. You deserve it," said Mr. Rohn. With tears welling up in his eyes, Jack thanked Mr. Rohn.

Mr. Rohn motioned towards the microphone. Jack stepped up to the microphone and looked over the vast crowd of his fellow sales champions. His eyes connected with Digger's. Digger gave him the thumbs up.

Jack began to speak, "Thank you. Thank you. I am not sure what to say. I am a little overwhelmed. But let me say this, it wasn't that long ago that I was sitting on a bench in total despair when everything changed. That was the day my mentor showed up. He planted a seed in my life that has turned into a plant of Sales Success. My friends, you never know when and where that seed will begin to grow. But if you want it, badly enough, it will grow...because you will grow. Hear me when I say, if I can do it...then you can do it! Sales Success is yours. Choose it. Take it. Live it!"

22 Minutes Later

Jack was exhausted...at least emotionally. He walked out of the auditorium and the first eyes he saw were those crystal blue eyes of Digger. "Well done, my boy," said Digger. "I am so proud of you!"

"Thank you Digger. I owe you so much."

With a wave of his hand Digger said, "Eh, you had it inside you all the time."

A short pause filled the expansive hallway. As they locked eyes, Jack finally realized... "You are leaving, aren't you Digger?"

"I have my new assignment. Besides, you don't need me anymore. You can fly on your own."

"I am going to miss you my friend," said Jack. With that, the two sales champions embraced as brothers.

As Digger turned and began to walk away, Jack called after him, "You know, you never did tell me who you really are!"

Digger paused, turned around, and with that trademark grin said, "Well, let me put it this way, my golfing buddy is Gabriel." He took a couple of steps and then added with a chuckle, "And, he has never beaten me yet. You know, I am pretty good."

With that, Digger walked down the hallway. Jack stood and watched his mentor, friend…brother. As Digger got further away, he faded, and faded, and faded, till he had disappeared. Jack smiled and walked towards the door…and his future.

About the Authors

MARK BOWSER

Mark Bowser is the author of several inspiring books including Sell Your Way to Success and Nehemiah on Leadership. Mark is the President/CEO of Empowering Enterprises, Inc which helps their clients create more income through increased sales and customer loyalty.

Since 1993, Mark has presented thousands of seminars as one of the United States top Motivational Business Speakers. He lives in the Cincinnati area with his wife and three children.

ZIG ZIGLAR

The late Zig Ziglar was a motivational speaker, teacher and trainer who traveled the world over delivering his messages of humor, hope, and encouragement. As a world renowned author and speaker, Zig had an appeal that transcended barriers of age, culture and occupation. From 1970 until 2010, he traveled over five million miles across the world delivering powerful life improvement messages, cultivating the energy of change. Recognized by his peers as the quintessential motivational genius of our times, Zig Ziglar's unique delivery style and powerful messages earned him many honors, and today he is still considered one of the most versatile authorities on the science of human potential.

Mr. Ziglar wrote over thirty celebrated books on personal growth, leadership, sales, faith, family and success, including *Born to Win*, *See You at the Top*, *Developing the Qualities of Success*, *Raising Positive Kids in a*

Negative World, Top Performance, Courtship After Marriage, Over The Top, and *Secrets of Closing the Sale*. Nine titles have been on the best seller lists; his books and audios have been translated into over thirty-eight languages and dialects. Zig Ziglar was a committed family man, dedicated patriot, and an active church member.

TOM HOPKINS

Tom Hopkins is world-renowned as The Builder of Sales Champions. His selling skills and sales strategies have helped millions of sales professionals and business owners in industries from A to Z to serve more clients, make more sales and earn millions in income.

Tom got his start in real estate sales when he was just 19 years of age. After an initial period of abject failure, he started learning the communication skills that made him the #1 real estate agent in the US within 7 years.

Since 1976 he has been teaching others his simple, yet powerful strategies and tactics through live events, books, CDs and video. Millions have turned their cars into classrooms, listening to Tom's advice on the way to appointments with potential new clients.

His client list includes the likes of AFLAC, 24 Hour Fitness, Best Buy, State Farm Insurance, Kavo, Eli Lilly, REMAX and many others. He also offers live public seminars in cities throughout the world.

Tom has authored 18 books including: *How to Master the Art of Selling, Selling for Dummies and his latest release, When Buyers Say No*.

DR. TONY ALESSANDRA

A former graduate professor of marketing, Dr. Tony Alessandra earned his PhD in marketing in 1976 and has published 14 books in 17 foreign languages. As an entrepreneur, he is president of AssessmentBusinessCenter.com, co-founder of MentorU.com and Chairman of BrainX.com. Recognized by Meetings & Conventions Magazine as "one of America's most electrifying speakers," he was inducted into the Speakers Hall of Fame in 1985.

DAWN JONES

Dawn Jones is an international speaker, corporate trainer and the best-selling author of the Top 7 Personality Challenges. After more than 20 years of corporate and entrepreneurial experience, she knows the secrets to success inside out.

As a professional speaker, Dawn is passionate about helping people reach their goals and live their dreams; as well as helping them discover the essentials of communicating for results, building self-esteem, and unlocking their paths to success.

Her fast-paced delivery, sprinkled with impacting stories and anecdotes, makes her one of the most stimulating and sought-after speakers in her specialty areas. Dawn addresses eager audiences both LIVE and on audio and DVD. Her corporate travels have taken her to Australia, New Zealand, England, and across North America. Her recently published recordings include Taking Control of Time and Priorities and Organizing Your Work and Life and Conflict Management Skills for Women as well as compilations with Zig Ziglar, Chris Widener, and Les Brown.

In her free time Dawn travels with her husband to East Africa where they volunteer with non-profit groups to help build a hope and a future for the next generation.

More than a theorist, Dawn has put her insights and methods to the test over and over in real-life situations, both professionally and personally. They are easy to implement. They work. And when combined, they create a concrete road map people can use to triumph over obstacles in their life and achieve their goals.

BRYAN HEATHMAN

If eCommerce is the new buzz word in today's business climate, Bryan Heathman wrote the book - literally! Hailed as the thought leader on Internet Conversion Marketing, Heathman shares his wealth of experience running more than 150 marketing campaigns for industry giants like Proctor & Gamble, AT&T, Microsoft, Travelocity, Lycos, and Nissan Motors. Few people have truly harnessed the magic of the Internet, but this acclaimed speaker has blazed the trail, from building a definitive customer list to optimizing your website for sales revenues. Get the key trade secrets from this entertaining and insightful industry insider.

ALLAN COLMAN

As CEO of the Closers Group, a business development advisory, Allan Colman has spent more than two decades helping law firms and professional service firms generate more revenue. He has brought in millions of dollars of new business and built business development structures that continue to perform. His clients call him their MENTOR/TORMENTOR.

Allan is known for his passion in developing pioneering strategies and for his ability to help clients generate business rapidly. He has spent many years listening to in-house counsel and business executives make decisions. Allan understands their reasoning for selecting outside professionals, and has also worked closely with law firms as they select their own advisors and consultants.

Allan holds Masters and Doctorate degrees from New York University. He is a pro bono mediator for the California Court of Appeals and the Los Angeles County Superior Court. His community activities have included Board positions with the Children's Cancer Research Fund, Los Angeles Council of Boy Scouts of America, Rotary Foundation and California Medical Center Foundation. He was awarded the "Masada Samurai Warrior" in 2004 by Masada Homes honoring his pro-bono work. He has served on the Board of Editors for Marketing the Law Firm and has a featured blog, The Red Zone, on the Law Journal Newsletters home page. Professional articles he has written and co-written have appeared in Bloomberg Law Management, National Law Journal, Los Angeles Business Journal, Diversity & the Bar, Los Angeles Daily Journal, Strategies, Of Counsel, Minnesota Bench and Bar, Law 360. Etc.

Allan has been a featured speaker at firm-wide events and practice area groups as diverse as Burt Hill (Architects and Engineers), Price Waterhouse Coopers, Mississippi and Rhode Island Bar Associations, Legal Marketing Association, American Institute of CPA's, Federal Defense and Corporate Counsel, Minority Corporate Counsel Association, National Hispanic Bar Association, and companies such as DuPont, Employers' Reinsurance Co., General Electric and Sears. His webinars on business development have been held by several professional associations.

SCOTT MCKAIN

Scott McKain is an internationally known authority who helps organizations create distinction in every phase of business and teaches the "Ultimate Customer Experience."

Scott McKain's keynote presentations benefit from three decades of experience, combined with his innate talent for articulating successful ideas. McKain has spoken before and consulted for the world's most influential corporations.

Scott McKain creates captivating presentations and bestselling books which clearly reveal how to create more compelling connections between you and your customers and how to stand out and move up, regardless of the economic climate in your industry.

Scott is the founder of a consulting and training company that explores the role of ultimate customer experiences in creating enhanced client retention and revenue, and is the author of three Amazon.com #1 business bestsellers; all teaching how to expand profits, increase sales, and engage customers. McKain's latest book, released by publisher McGraw-Hill and titled 7 Tenets of Taxi Terry, provides the specific steps for every employee to create and deliver ultimate customer experiences.

He has presented his business strategies on platforms in all fifty states and seventeen countries...from Singapore to Sweden; from Mexico to Morocco... from the White House with the President in attendance; to conferences in Dubai and Abu Dhabi. He has been honored with induction into the "Professional Speakers Hall of Fame." And, he is a member of "Speakers Roundtable" — an elite, invitation-only group of twenty business speakers considered by many to be among the best in the world.

More Best Selling Sales & Success Books

So, You're New To Sales
By Bryan Flanagan

Every day scores of people enter the sales field. Some are young, some are more mature, but most have never studied the art of selling and few know where to begin. So, You're New to Sales takes all the guesswork out of how to become a skilled professional salesperson.

From learning how to identify your prospect to helping them get what they need, this book covers all the steps necessary to expertly deliver a sales presentation

Sales Success

with confidence that you can handle every question, every objection, and have the best closing ratio possible.

Bryan Flanagan will help you understand the extreme responsibility the salesperson has to be trustworthy, reliable, resourceful, and proud of the profession by helping others find solutions to their needs.

Few opportunities offer the ability to write your own paycheck, but working on a sales commission is one of them! Apply the principles Bryan teaches and be amazed as you see how selling simply is a formula you apply. You don't have to have what some consider "a salesman's personality," you just have to "know how to sell" and have the desire to make your life what YOU want it to be!

Sell it Today, Sell it Now
By Tom Hopkins

Have you discovered the power of the one-call close? *Sell it Today, Sell it Now* by sales champion, **Tom Hopkins**, is your ultimate reference guide to planning and perfecting the art of one-call closing. Whether you are an established sales professional with a long track record of achievement or a newcomer yet to make that first sale, you will learn why hundreds of thousands of salespeople use this book as a resource for new techniques and surprising insights.

You will discover how easy it is to:

- Employ the 15 keys of overcoming objections
- Overcome your fear of closing
- Manage the 4 concepts that control all sales
- Let your customers answer their own objections
- Master the art of the one-call close

Once you get a taste of this easy-going, soft-selling, results-only-system, you'll absolutely love it and never want to sell any other way. This step-by-step sales training book holds the key to your successful sales career.

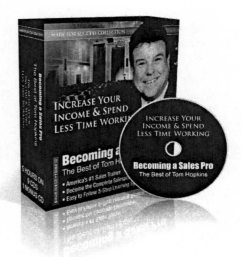

Becoming a Sales Pro
Featuring Tom Hopkins

You want to be in the top percentage of income-earners in your company. In order to do that, you need to learn what the top pros know and how they work. Master sales trainer Tom Hopkins has been building sales champions for years. Learn how to handle normal sales stress factors, how to communicate better with your clients, overcome objections and close more sales by using the right words and phrases. This nine-part audio series can help you learn and utilize the skills necessary to push yourself and others to the top of the business ladder.

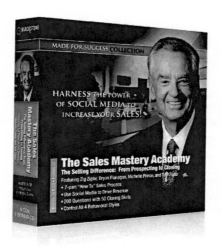

Sales Mastery Academy
Featuring Zig Ziglar

Learn to harness the power of social media to increase your sales! In this nine-part audio is a proven step-by-step process to guide you through the evolution of the sales profession. Learn how to set and achieve your goals with Zig Ziglar's unique seven-step goal attainment procedure, and learn the fundamental skills to meeting the changes with prospects and customers.

Rapid technological changes in the workplace have created new demands for sales professionals. Now that the world is flat from a sales territory viewpoint, cross cultural negotiation abilities have created a need for a new skill set in the world of selling. *The Sales Mastery Academy* has the answers, including sales prospecting skills, negotiation techniques, foolproof closing methods from the Master Closer, overcoming objections with the LQET formula, and of course, how to get and stay motivated. The concepts and skills outlined by three of the most sought after experts in their field will enable you to arrive with confidence and comfort.

Includes 1 bonus PDF workbook!

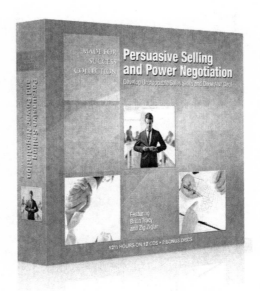

Persuasive Selling and Power Negotiation
Featuring Brian Tracy, Zig Ziglar, Laura Stack and more

Become naturally persuasive and improve the quality of your life!

Did you know that everything is negotiable? Unfortunately, most people are poor negotiators, and the number one reason why can be traced back to early childhood. This audio series can help you change that. Whether you are trying to influence or negotiate with your largest client, boss, spouse or even one of your children -- you need to be skillful. Do you think it might help to be better at reading body language? Would it be beneficial to know how to overcome the most frequently occurring miscommunication problem? Would knowing exactly how someone can be persuaded, be helpful in your interactions? Well now you can! Listen as the experts reveal their secrets so you, too, can succeed.

Includes
DVD: Zig Ziglar Sales Mastery System
PDF Workbook: Zig Ziglar Sales Mastery Workbook
   An Authoritative Look at Motivation by the World's #1 Motivator

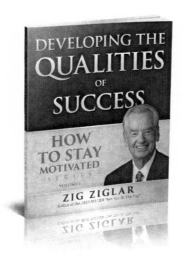

How to Stay Motivated
An Authoritative Look at Motivation by the World's #1 Motivator

How to Stay Motived: Developing the Qualities of Success was created with a focus on helping people succeed. Zig had a passion for helping people become their best and this program was designed to help you grow personally and professionally in four critical areas: qualities, abilities, skills, and attitudes.
By focusing on these 4 core areas, you gain characteristics of success, professionalism, excellence, and perhaps the very best return of all: improved overall performance. Developing the Qualities of Success will cover:

1. Planning, preparing and expecting to win
2. Taking the first step to a brighter future
3. Motivation, the key to accomplishment
4. Identifying the qualities of success
5. Developing the qualities of success
6. Maintaining a winning attitude

In this valuable program Zig encourages you to remember, "You were designed for accomplishment. You were engineered for success. You were endowed with the seeds of greatness." Apply these winning steps from the motivational master himself to build a better, more productive and satisfying life for yourself and what you do for yourself will naturally extend to your family. Developing the qualities of success will help you maintain your motivation, through all the ups and downs of life. Join millions who have used the success principles from Zig Ziglar and we will see you at the top!

CPSIA information can be obtained at www.ICGtesting.com
Printed in the USA
LVOW11s1950170416

484033LV00001B/1/P